BEAR'S

NECESSITIES

A 'SIMPLE GUIDE TO LIFE

SJH PUBLISHING

To all those women who have dreamed
of making the side bar of the Mail Online
and to the guys who want to be with them.

CONTENTS

Unit 1	School	9
Unit 2		9
Unit 3	Health	27
Unit 4	Food	
Unit 5	Extreme Things	
Unit 6	Style	9
Unit 7	Celebrities	96
Unit 8		
Unit 9	Phenomena	
Unit 10	Personal Experience	109
Unit 11	Emotions	118
Unit 12	Sport	139
Unit 14	Family	153
Unit 15	The Media	160
Unit 16	Education	171
Unit 17	The Future of Entertainment	188

CONTENTS

Unit 1:   School Days   9

Unit 2:   Jobs   19

Unit 3:   Travelling and Life Building   35

Unit 4:   Your First Taste of The Action   56

Unit 5:   Ex on The Beach   62

Unit 6:   Style   79

Unit 7:   Celebrity Big Brother   88

Unit 8:   Girls   104

Unit 9:   Planning for The Future   121

Unit 10:   Personal Appearances   126

Unit 11:   Ambitions   135

Unit 12:   Social Media   146

Unit 14:   Family   154

Unit 15:   The Media   169

Unit 16:   Bearligion   174

Unit 17:   Things You Never Knew About Bear   183

THAT'S ME!

A WORD FROM THE AUTHOR

As a guru on all things, I'm often asked what the key to my success is. The answer? Stay excited about life. Me, I'm always excited (and people can usually tell). Any project that comes my way, I grab by the horns and give it my best shot:

Going to school? **Exciting.**
Working on a roof? **Exciting.**
First girlfriend? **So exciting. (Sometimes got overexcited.)**
Travelling to Australia? **Yeah! Exciting mate.**
Going on telly for the first time? **Exciting!**
Winning *Celebrity Big Brother*? **The most exciting thing ever**

There are many reasons – including staying excited about things – that have meant I've been able to make my own way in life, and in this book I tell you all about my journey right up to where I am now, this very minute, eating a packet of crisps. I also give you the best tips on how to make your own way and a success of your life. So if you want a gold star in the School of Life (which, unless you're an idiot, you should), read this book. Just sit back, relax and learn from the guru …

UNIT 1: SCHOOL DAYS

In this chapter you will get to grips with how to behave at school and how not to behave at school – with Bear giving detailed examples of both from personal experience. You will gain in-depth knowledge about the solar system, and discover why Bear used to call one of his teachers "Mr Ballbags".

The chapter concludes with Bear's top tips on how to survive school, cheat well, do your homework and do your best. You are encouraged to put what you have learned into practice at the end of this and each subsequent chapter.

BEAR ON SCHOOL

One of my first memories is this photo. I'm only six years old and I'm already poking my tongue out at my teacher – that picture sums me up to a tee. I was always getting told off at school, mostly because I was always talking (and that pretty much sums up my school days). But regardless, I loved school, absolutely loved it. I went to St Saviour's C of E School – a church school for modest, good little boys like me. The logo on the school jumpers was an owl in a hat (pretty cool). Once a week we'd follow our teachers up to the local church – walking hand-in-hand – and we'd have to sit through a service. Afterwards, we would have communion and do the whole "handshaking-peace-be-with-you" thing, which I liked. But I remember this one day I got into some real, serious trouble: I was about eight at the time, and just as someone went to shake my hand and say, "peace be with you," I held out my hand, and as they did the same I snatched mine away and ran my hands through my hair like John Travolta in *Grease* – like, "Aaah … so smooth." Ultimately, it wasn't that smooth because I got sent to Miss Hawes' office and she went nuts. She actually made me cry, it was totally ruthless. I was never naughty in church again after that. I was also worried that Jesus would tell Santa, and then Santa would scratch me off his "good kid" list. I just wasn't prepared to take that risk.

Post "handshake-gate" I may have stopped any funny business inside church but I was still cheeky everywhere else, and personally I think that's the best way of getting through school: having fun. So if you're in school now, just keep people laughing and capture people's attention. Be memorable. You want to be the kid that gets brought up in conversation time and time again at the pub when you're older:

"Do you remember that time Bear flicked a bogey in your lunchbox?"

"Yeah, it was amazing."

That's the person you want to be – they just didn't get my humour at the time, which, ultimately, is their loss. But I never said naughty words or anything like that (even though I knew them all); I was just the class clown. And even though they'd never admit it, I could just tell my teachers loved me. I think they used to talk fondly of me in that staffroom every day of the week; they probably even raised glasses and gave toasts in my name, thanking me for keeping them entertained ... maybe they had a shrine. (I actually don't know where they found their patience.)

There was a teacher called Mr Glampson, he taught Geography and everyone called him "Ballbags" because it looked like he had ball bags under his eyes – which was unfortunate for the poor fella, in hindsight. But I always remember something he said to me. In his class, I always put my hand up – not because I was being annoying, but because I kept thinking of things to ask, and he didn't seem to mind. Then one day he asked everyone, "Why do you all laugh every time Stephen Bear asks a question?" The whole class was silent, no one answered. I thought he was going to say something horrible about me, but then he said, "If you don't ask questions, you'll never learn any answers." It was great to hear such a nice compliment. He said, "I like it when Stephen asks questions because it means he wants to learn." I've always remembered that, and I've asked questions ever since, like: Where am I? What day is it? Don't you know who I am? – that kind of thing.

Still, my favourite teacher loved me and I had her wrapped round my little finger. Other kids would often join my silliness, and I'd always catch her cracking up a little bit, but trying to cover it up. That's the trick: to make the teachers laugh if you can, but not out loud – just in their head. Back then I'd be a little cheeky chops without being offensive to anyone, and it's stayed one of my personality traits throughout my life: be naughty, not rude. I did that loads in the *Big Brother* house (so you can watch that to see how it's done). Anyone who thinks I'm horrible just doesn't get me. I like EVERYONE and I always want to make people laugh, especially if it's someone I think doesn't like me – I make a special effort for those people. They need my love.

Because I was (generally) a good little boy, I tried to learn, I really did – even when I got home from school. My mum, Linda, would sit me and my brother Rob at the table and make us do our homework. I never missed one piece of homework – partly because my mum always used to help me (every. single. night.). But somehow I'd always end up remembering weird stuff no one else did, and then forget the main bits. But if someone shows me something that's hands-on, that's a totally different story – I learn it straight away, which is probably why I've always loved drawing, so I obviously did well in art. Even now, I like watching Disney films and doing my drawings (they are mad and mainly cartoon characters like Sonic The Hedgehog and Bart Simpson). When I was little and my mum needed to keep me quiet, she would always give me a pen and paper to draw something. It always worked; I'd sit there for hours. It's very calming, I can still get lost in it. I've got a whole book filled with doodles, and I actually won a competition in the *Celebrity Big Brother* house for my abstract work; because with art, I think outside the box and, without even trying, I'm a genius.

In primary school, my mates and me made up a gang. We called ourselves "The Cool Gang". We wanted to show that we were all members of the gang by doing something distinctive, and we'd noticed that in the library there was a yellow card in every book. So, I stole eight of the yellow cards from the books, made them into what I called "Cool Cards" and gave them to all my friends.

We thought that we were the best, but there was a boy we were friends with, Daniel Davies, who, when he heard about the gang and wasn't in it, started crying, "I want to be in it the gang." So I said, "Calm down Daniel, calm down," and I tore my Cool Card in half so he could join. I am kind like that, and he really, really wanted to be in the gang.

I might have gone to the library to nick the yellow cards but I've never read a book. Ever. Not a single book. I read Biff, Chip and Kipper in infant school, but I just can't absorb the information in most books – I get bored. If someone is saying something to me, I can't really take it in and it's the same with newspapers; my mum is always nagging me saying, "You need to know what's going on in the world." I do get it's important, but I always feel like I'm wasting my time. I catch snippets here and there, but I don't follow current affairs as such because I can't concentrate on what the person on the news is saying. It is on my bucket list to learn Spanish, though; it would be nice to live out in Ibiza and actually be able to speak the lingo with the locals. I think it's a nice gesture to try and converse in the language of the country you're in, especially if you live there, but if you just go about speaking your own language, it seems a bit rude to me. As I don't read books, I suppose I'll have to learn it via audiobook.

At secondary school, which was called Holy Family Catholic School, I started to take sport a bit more seriously and became captain of the football team. I was always getting other kids to join in; but, unluckily for them, I was always the one to score the goals. At 24, I got a football trial for Wealdstone and trained really hard. Then, a week before the trial, I had a run-in with the goalie and did my ankle in. I didn't think it was that bad at the time, but it turned out it was worse than anyone expected. I was laid up for an entire year with that injury so the trial never happened. But it was that year I got the offer for *Ex On The Beach* so it wasn't all bad – though I'd still love to have been a footballer.

I was always better at the physical stuff at school than the written stuff. Out of all the subjects, Geography was my worst, closely followed by RE – I used to count the seconds until that one ended. I knew how to get to the West End and Hackney Wick, and that there was God in the world, so I didn't feel there was a need to elaborate on that knowledge.

Still, I worked hard, but however much homework I did, my reports always said the same thing: that I was the class joker. But I couldn't help that – it's just my nature. I was never a spiteful kid, though. I didn't like bullies and I would always try to stick up for any kids that were having a hard time. I like helping people, that's also in my nature, and I think it's a great mindset to have. Helping others is the one thing that my mum and dad have always been adamant about – just be nice, and you'll find the world will be nice back to you. I do believe in karma, it's definitely worked out well for me … so far.

When it was time for school tests, I'd find someone clever to copy off. At least, that's what I'd try to do. I once copied Rachel Downey's science test – I'd already snogged Rachel in a game of spin the bottle. We were in Year 8 and that was my first kiss – I remember that she had lip-gloss on, which felt funny. The bottle landed on me, then her, then everyone counted to ten and we had to snog for the whole time. I got a really bad headache afterwards, but I must have been quite good at kissing for her to let me copy her work. Unfortunately for me, her work wasn't up to my snogging, and she got a really easy question wrong, which I copied. It was: "If the Earth orbits the Sun, what does the Moon orbit?" She wrote down, "the Sun", and so did I, when obviously it should have been "the Earth". It was such a stupid answer that it was obvious that I had copied her work. I couldn't believe it! How could she have written "the Sun"? I was embarrassed for her really. And also me. I never copied Rachel's exam answers ever again. However, I did copy another classmate's, Simon's, math tests. He would help me by putting his work to one side (my side), so that's probably why I did well in those.

In my GCSEs I did well in sport, but that was a given because I was a natural. Overall, I got five Cs and four Ds. Of course, I know they're not great results, but I didn't care about them even back then. I always knew I was going to work for myself, and be massive in whatever I did, obviously. I knew that my GCSEs wouldn't help me; what I wanted to do was something that only I could achieve. So, I needed to take some time out to work out what it was I wanted to do – with my brain power and drive for success, I knew I'd be okay if I tried my hardest.

Hang on, does the Moon orbit the Earth? Is that right?

BEARZY'S TOP TIPS FOR GETTING THROUGH SCHOOL

Listen up! School is so important. Getting through school is something I always tell kids to do. See it through to the end and try your hardest the whole way through. Do your homework and get it in on time. Ask your mum to help, or your dad, or your sister, your uncle, your dog – it doesn't matter who, just get your homework done and get it in on time. Really, you should have friends who are willing to help if you are a decent person. Copy their work as and when needed. If someone else that you know has a class before yours with the same teacher in the same room, quickly ask to see their tests, because you know you'll probably be doing the same one when you get in there and try to quickly scan through them to memorise a few cheeky answers.

If you want to make life easy for yourself, though, try to pay attention during lessons. Take notes in class to make sure you've understood the lesson (I never did this but wish I had). You'll be in trouble when it is exam time otherwise, trust me. Like I've already said, I tried to ask a lot of questions – although sometimes I did that just to keep me awake, which was more than some kids managed. The teachers are teachers for reasons – they're probably better than your friends at explaining things. You're stuck in the shit room for an hour or so anyway, so you might at least make some use of the time.

If you learn in class, you don't have to waste time on homework outside of school and you can knock around with your mates instead, play Pokémon Go, climb a tree, or whatever it is you want to do.

But, and this is a big but (I cannot lie, you other brothers can't deny) – if there's something you're the best at – DO THAT. If you're great at writing, don't bother with your times tables. If you're great at art, don't bother with chemistry. Who cares about the stuff that you haven't got a talent for. Do the things that make you tick, because that is what life is really about when it comes down to it. In other words: learn only what's important for you to know. Don't waste time with things you don't give a shit about. For example, if you get stuck on something in maths, and for some reason can't get the answer to a problem, think to yourself, "Do I really need to know this?" Try to understand it and work it out, if you can, because then you'll find it eventually gets easier to work out what you need to know versus what you don't, and what you just can't be bothered to figure out.

And lastly, remember: at school and in life, not everyone is going to like you; but I promise that doesn't matter. Just plough through it, be kind even to the unkind people. And never be rude to your teachers. In fact, never be rude – no need! You'll always come out on top in the end.

Please note: I'm not genuinely advising you to give your homework to your dog – unless it's Geography or something. Otherwise, it's probably better to ask someone who won't eat it.

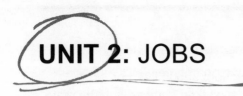

UNIT 2: JOBS

This chapter gives you a detailed overview of Bear's first experiences of employment and how to jump from one job to the next if you've got some good banter. In this chapter you will also find out what the "liquor" surrounding pie and mash is made from (hint: eels), how to handle a crisis and how to make a killing when you throw a party.

Includes: *Bear's tips on how to save money once you've earned it, why you shouldn't just "spunk" your whole pay packet, and how to motivate yourself to put in the effort to succeed.*

Please note: *In practice, students should make sure they get permission before they start throwing any parties.*

BEAR ON JOBS

I was 15 when I got my first job, in Manze's pie and mash shop on Walthamstow market. Pie and mash is a traditional working-class food from London, and you cannot beat it – Manze's is one of the most famous pie and mash shops, too. Traditionally, the shops have white tile walls with mirrors, and marble floors, tables, and worktops – all of which are easy to clean. (They call them shops not restaurants for some reason, and I've always wondered about that.)

L.Manze in Walthamstow is typical old-school style and they've kept it as it would have been in Victorian times – it's a Grade II listed building now. One day, I just walked in there with my mate John, and said, "Have you got any Saturday jobs?" The owners said they might, took down both of our phone numbers and said they'd be in touch – so we were both expecting to get a job. But later that evening they rang my house to tell me that I'd got the job, and John hadn't. I didn't feel bad – I knew I'd get it if it came down to it; plus I don't think John was bothered either way. The next Saturday, I went in for my first shift; I would be getting paid £30 a day to wipe tables and clean plates away mostly. It was all going really well until a few hours in to the shift when Jonathan's mum marched in (with him in tow), totally furious that I'd got the job and not him. She shouted, "Where's Stephen? My Jonathan should have got that job over him!" John didn't care that I was working there and he wasn't, but he did care his mum hadn't taken it well – he was so embarrassed. It's continues to be a running joke between us because John's mum is still like that – honestly, Ant and Dec were lucky she didn't run over that bridge screaming, "My lovely Jonathan should have won over that Stephen!"

The food at Manze's pie and mash shop is amazing still – go down there for your lunch when you're next in the area. They've got liquor, jellied eels, the works. If you don't know what "liquor" in a pie and mash shop is, let me tell you – it's the bollocks. It's not booze, to start with, so don't go thinking it's some kind of vodka jelly. What it is is you get mashed potato to spread around one side of the plate, then on the other side, you get this little puddle of green stuff, which is the liquor. What it's made from might sound disgusting: it's eel liquor sauce, as in the slippery eels from the river. It's made using the water kept from the stewed eels, which pie and mash shops also sell. That's the proper East End traditional way, though there are a lot of shops that no longer use real stewed eel water in their liquor because people feel a bit grossed out by it I think. Instead of the eel water, they make the puddle green by just using parsley sauce made with an Oxo cube or something; which is definitely not the same or going to taste anywhere near as good. I still absolutely love traditional liquor, and the shop. But in my heart, I knew I didn't want to work in shops or cafes forever (or, in fact, for more than three weeks).

My eldest brother, Danny, was a businessman and he was my inspiration. Not just because he never did well in school either and had to retake his exams, but because he was such a good businessman. When I'd come home from the shop in the evening, I'd see him collapsed on the sofa absolutely knackered. It sounds mad, but I wanted to feel like he did after putting in a full day's graft. I wanted to be "business tired". I didn't want to do a normal office job and climb the ladder; I wanted to be the one to put the ladder out there, regardless of whether there was a wall behind it or not, or even if there was anyone willing to climb it. I just knew I wanted to be in charge of my own goddamn ladder.

The first step towards this was quitting my job at the pie and mash shop – it just wasn't my thing (I could see all my mates going out and I was jealous). But because I was already such a good businessman, I had another job lined up. I'd gone to see Spurs play with my brother and we'd had a really good day, I was feeling pumped so when we got to the shop on the grounds I asked, "Got any jobs mate?" Turned out he did. He took my number and rang me after a couple of days, saying I could start work; and that is how business is done, my friend.

My life's basically just been a series of promotions ever since. Like my next job when I was 16, which was in the merchandise store at Tottenham Hotspur FC. Initially, I had to pack all the hangers up and straighten out the stuff on the shelves. Eventually they trusted me on the tills, and I was amazing with the customers ('course I was): "You having a nice day? Where did you come from today? Your smile just brightened up my week!" all that stuff – customers like a bit of banter. But one time I was struggling to remove a plastic security tag, I was wrestling with it for a bit at the till, and this guy said, "God, I hope that Tottenham play faster than this." That really mugged me off. I only lasted five weeks there.

I got a new job when I was looking for clothes in Abercrombie and Fitch. I wanted full-time work by then because I'd left school, so I decided to ask them if they were looking for anyone and they were (me!). They hired me a week later (which I think probably had something to do with the fact that I walked in looking so fresh, because I always look fresh) and I quickly became the king of "clothes folding". I was insanely good at it, like a machine. Every time someone touched them, I'd refold; sometimes I'm sure they'd refold just by me looking at them. I can still do super-mega folding now. Just ask me to fold something, and I can fold the shit out of it. But I only stayed there five weeks, as well. I just get bored so quickly – happens when you're really good at stuff.

In my heart, I knew I still wanted to be outdoors doing something physical. So after finding out about a roofing course at Barking College, I enrolled and would get the bus to Harold Hill every day, sitting on the top deck (like a legend). I remember on my first day of college, I walked down from the top deck, thinking I was looking pretty cool and everyone was admiring me. As it turned out, I had a lump of chewing gum stuck to my bum, leaving a long, long string of it stretching down the stairs – like if Spider Man's bum leaked. It was so bad. After a start like that, I didn't know whether I'd get along there or not; but despite the risk of me being called "leaky spider bum", I got my qualification to be a roofer, as well as an NVQ in plumbing. I passed my NVQ1 easily, but to do my level 2, I needed to get an apprenticeship and go to college at the same time – hard-core. So I rang up my friend Mark, who's uncle, Paul, ran a company, and he said he'd let me work for him. During that period I learned many things, including how to work with zinc and lead pipes used in boilers, which was fascinating (not).

After finishing college, I got an apprenticeship to carry on training to be a roofer – and I LOVED it. I got paid £40 a day and I'd get up at 6:15 in the morning to be on the roof at 8am. For a year-and-a-half, I really knuckled down and tried to concentrate, but I was still getting loads of ideas and I wanted a finger in every single pie … and pasty, and doughnut, sausage roll, iced bun – in fact, I wanted my fingers in all delicious baked goods. And then I wanted to eat them.

In all seriousness, I think this is really the key to getting started. You need to try a few things out – you should never settle for the first job you find (unless it's astronaut). How do you ever know what's out there for you if you don't try different things?

One of the things I tried out was this wicked idea that I knew would take off: Aussie-style beach parties! I know, amazing. But imagine a time without Instagram, Twitter or Snapchat – back then MySpace was just starting to die and Facebook was the only social media site to sniff about on. Still, I knew enough people in East London that if I could tap into inviting people on Facebook, I'd be onto a winner. I bought some mad inflatables, rubber rings, animals, that sort of thing, and went off to B&Q to buy some sun-loungers, as well as a load of bags of sand, palm trees, whistles; and low and behold, I had Bondi Beach in the back of a van.

With half of Australia in my van, I went down to the E10 club – where I knew the owners – near my home in Hackney. No one went there ever – maybe around three people a week or something rubbish like that. It was dead, and even the three people who were there were probably dead. So I told them I could pack the place out with people – and it was true, I knew loads of people in East London, and beyond. I rang everyone I knew who still had a heartbeat and started promoting it: "Come down, it'll be the best party ever," I told them.

In the end, I swapped the venue because E10 couldn't make up their minds quick enough about how awesome the party was going to be, and my first beach party packed out the new venue. My dad was taking the money on the door, charging £10 a ticket. I borrowed my mum's deckchairs, as well, but they got broken and she wasn't very happy. But ultimately that didn't matter either because it was the most MASSIVE thing ever. Except for when I did the same thing later on at Club Warehouse in Chingford, and then in Blue Mondays club in Chingford, that really was the most massive thing ever. At Blue Mondays they had to shut the bar because they ran out of drink during one of my nights. Actually shut the bar, imagine that! At the time, I was doing that and still roofing. I was trying to juggle both and getting told off by my boss because I was always on a phone call, trying to arrange the next big do. It was hard work doing both, but as usual, I pulled it off.

This is the thing about crises; we all have them, but it's about how you keep your cool and handle it. Like this example: I'd sold all the tickets, but I had nowhere to put the party on. "You're screwed, just cancel it," my mates said. But no way was I giving up because I knew my idea was a winner. In business, especially new businesses, you've got to expect the dramas, and then you've got to plough through them like a raging bull. It pays off – on my 21st birthday, I went to Newz Bar in Liverpool. I got off with a girl who said she was Steven Gerrard's cousin, but I reckon every girl in there used that line.

My ambitions, however, are greater than wanting to snog Steven Gerrard's cousin, anyway: I want to be bigger than Alan Sugar. You think he's got a lot of money? He's got nothing. I want to be on the Forbes rich list at number one. I'm only 26, so I've got a lot of years left in me – certainly more than Sugar – and although I've got crazy, wacky, ideas, anything I put my head to just works out, so I don't see why I can't get to number one on the Forbes rich list.

He may not be at the top of the Forbes rich list, but Alan Sugar is definitely smarter than his American *The Apprentice* cousin, Donald Trump – he isn't clever, he just inherited all of his money from his mum and dad, that's how clever he is (not very clever, but he is the President of America). Honestly, I'm going to go for presidency now. If he can do it, I don't see why I can't. I could also be the Prime Minster of England. Or the King. There's plenty of time …

Anyway, my presidency's probably a few years off yet and Kanye's got to have a crack at it first, so for now I'm focusing on my brand, East End Clobber – this is my baby. The website is www.eastendclobber.com and I chose that name because, obviously, I'm from the East End. I've started off making hats, but I want to progress onto shorts, t-shirts, swimwear, aftershave, watches, a women's range, kids' range, bed sheets, pillowcases, trainers, condoms, hair gel, hair brushes, picture frames, light bulbs, windows – you name it, I'll East End Clobber it.

Starting the company has been an interesting experience because the whole thing is mine, so I'm my own boss now. I've always wanted to be a businessman, always wanted to sell stuff, always said I'm going to have a business; and it has gone really well so far – I get people coming up to me saying, "Oh, I just bought one of your hats," and they can't wait for new colours to come out. It makes me feel really clever. I knew I was clever, but when people wear your merchandise and are genuinely excited about when your new stock is arriving, it brings a whole new edge to it: not only am I a businessman, I'm actually seen as a style icon, which is unbelievable

(especially when you read about what I used to wear in
the "Style" chapter).

The reason I started with hats first with East End Clobber
was simply because everyone wears hats. That might sound
ridiculous, but I got sent a free hat and put it on and thought,
"You know what, I'll have this exact same shape hat; but I want
to put my own logo on it and my own material." And that's exactly
how it started – I just copied the exact shape and started selling it
myself ("good artists copy, great artists steal").

A major lesson I've learned in business is you've got to be cruel to
be kind – but this is also the one area where I've gone wrong. My
brother Danny is a very successful businessman and he says, "Never
employ friends and never employ family." Well, I've employed my
sister to look after emails, and I've employed my other brother Robert
to do the packing – and already it's not going well.

Something else that's important to know if you're going to start
your own business is the value of your merchandise. It may
seem obvious, but you've got to know how much your stock is
worth, and how much to sell it for. Supposing you buy a hundred
hats at 3p, you don't want to sell your hats for 2p, that's running at
a loss. If you sold a hundred hats, you'd loose 100p altogether;
so imagine if your hats were bought for £30 and you sold them
at £20 – that's when you start losing serious money. So what
you want to do is start high, that's what I do. At first, my mum
said, "You're mad, who's going to pay £30 for a hat?" But they
do, because I'm giving the illusion of expensiveness. I never,
ever, ever want to do a sale, because I think it would depreciate

Office

Bouncy Castt

Me working on my next projectl

Me at Desk

Stilt walker

T.V

Bed with girls in

My next plan is to save up for a helecopter.

helecopter.

the value of my brand. Instead, do you know what I've done?
I've brought my hats out in new colours, and I'm selling them for
£50, and their selling. People might think I'm mad – £50 for a
hat – but some of these hats are going for $250, and people are
paying for them. So now I want to keep going up and up, and on
and on. Never undervalue your merchandise, don't devalue your
brand, ever. For me, that is key: keep stock, keep it high and
never, ever, ever give a discount – you don't see Giorgio Armani
selling their outfits for two quid down the market now do you?

I've got an office – don't act like you're not impressed. That's
pretty much the ultimate part about having your own business;
well, it is if you have an office like mine. When I first got it I was
told, "You can't change the carpet, you can't paint the walls
and you can't put blinds up." You know what I did? I got a new
carpet; I've the painted the walls, and I'm about to put some
electric blinds up. The way I see it is, no-one else is going to
pay for that space – it's been derelict for ages – so they're
lucky I'm in there. The theme for my office – well for room one,
the main room where I cut deals – is *Scarface*. It's really dark
– gold and black – and it's got a picture of Tony Montana on
the wall. It's got a big crushed-velvet sofa in there, there's a big
telly on the wall and the carpet is black with a red stripe running
through the middle of it. I've got my desk and chair there and
another desk where my sister Hailey sits. On the desks, I've got
these green lamps like they use in The Godfather – I bought
three of them off the internet. In front of the electric blinds that
are going to go up, I've got big crushed-velvet curtains. When
you open them, they've got big chunky gold ropes so they
drape down, which really sets off the look.

The reason for the whole "mafia" vibe is that when I have like a thousand different people working for me, I want them to knock on the door and come into my office and be a bit scared and worried as to what I'm going to tell them – it's the atmosphere you've got to create. The room next door is themed like the Joker because I love the Joker; so the colour scheme is purple and green. I've got purple blinds going in, I've got green blinds, I've got purple walls, I've got a purple pool table, I've got a black sofa in there, and if you remember the computer game *Street Fighter* then you'll appreciate the arcade machine that I'm putting in there. So it's just a room to go and chill out in. I've also got lava lamps, because it's where I cleanse – after I've cut a big, important business deal in the *Scarface* room, I go next door and play some pool. I guess I want the office to just be a home from home; it's just to get out the house and feel more like a businessman.

My mindset with regards to business, jobs and money is totally different from a few years ago – if I want a helicopter I'm not going to start selling things to get a helicopter, now I know I've just got to work really hard to keep what I've got, and then get a helicopter. When I've got a helicopter I could get some more money and I could try and build a spaceship, maybe go to Mars or Jupiter – I don't see why not. Why can't I build one? Just picture it now: "Bear In Space". Or will I get stopped by traffic control in the sky?

BEARZY'S TOP TIPS FOR GETTING A JOB

Write that shit down. Everything. I write down times, dates, everything. Where you went, why you went there, who was there. Not only is it useful for turning up on time – and on the right day – it also makes you look like a good businessperson. But mostly, it's important to write everything down so you can talk about it all later when you write a book (now, that's a tip to live by).

A lot of my success is down to the way my dad's bought me up; it's the perfect way to look at life. He doesn't care about anything except for his family and being kind to people – if he was down to his last tenner, he'd give you a fiver (a bit like me with my "Cool Cards"). He's taught me to make the most of life and take every opportunity, and that's helped me so much.

Another thing to bear in mind when you get a job is: it's important to pay your way, but it's just as important to save your money, too. The number of times I went out on the weekend and blew my entire week's pay packet makes me cringe now. I can't believe I didn't just put a little bit away every week, or even give it to

31

my mum to put away for me every week. I'd have been rich by the time I was 21 if I'd been more careful with my money and got a mortgage earlier in life; because I worked constantly, but I spunked all my money. When you get a job you love, work hard, and hold on to your money. Even if you don't love your job, keep working hard until you're in a position to get one that you do love. If you really want something, you can make it happen. Just remember to always hold on to your money.

Most people think that they need to be born with some sort of natural talent if they want to get into a certain business, or even to be an entrepreneur. But you don't need natural talent! You can learn everything you need if you're hungry enough for it. Being self-taught is alright for some, but I'd advise you learn from mentors, other entrepreneurs on YouTube and the people around you who are wise, so that you can get up to speed as quickly as possible. Then, once you are up to speed, you can start putting your own bit of flair on things. But bear in mind, some dickheads brag that they are "self taught" like it's a fucking gold star they were given by a teacher. Fuck that shit. All that really sounds like to people is that you don't know what you're talking about, so you are probably shit at it.

Next, let's get something straight: we all have 24 hours in a day – unless you are in space, then some freaky stuff happens. If you're not in space, everyone's day consists of the same amount of hours. Saying you "don't have time" is just bullshit. If you are alive, eating, sleeping, shitting – and not severely disabled – you have the same amount of time as I do, and everyone else does. You just choose to use your time differently. So if you're saying that you really don't have time to start a new business, you can buy more time by waking up one hour earlier. If you can't wake up one hour earlier, skip lunch and work on your new business while you eat. Remember, if anyone asks you, don't say you are unemployed – you're not out of work, you're just between jobs. Much more professional.

In business, I think you just have to go with your heart. If you think something is right, just go for it. But you also have to be prepared to fail – it doesn't matter, everyone fails. But to try and avoid it, I always aim to focus on the solutions, not the problems. For example: what are you going to do if something is not going right for one month? Suppose a lot of stock is not getting sold. What are you going to do? You might tell your friends, but your friends will probably laugh at you and tell you to just quit and give up. Instead, you need to think, why isn't it selling? What can I do to make this sell more? Who can I approach to maybe sell more?

On which note, it's worth remembering not to surround yourself with negative people, because when you start hanging out with negative people, you're asking for their advice, and they'll bring you down, bring you to their level, and it's embarrassing. You haven't got time for negativity, I'm afraid. It's all smiles!

And lastly, remember: you've got to be cruel to be kind.

UNIT 3: TRAVELLING AND LIFE BUILDING

This chapter will focus on equipping you with all the core skills required for any adventure; how to, and why you should, follow your intuition and inspiration; and why you should always keep a scrapbook. Students are advised to buy a scrapbook, and start it, in order to complete this chapter.

You will also learn about Bear's time in Australia, his brief period fruit picking and selling cheese door-to-door, and his advice on how drunk to be when talking to strangers in a foreign country. You will also learn how exactly how much fun Bear had in Thailand, how many lady-boys he met, and why you should be aware of good vibes and bad vibes in a new country.

Includes: *Bear's top tips on how you can replicate the good times he had – and avoid the pitfalls.*

Please note: *Students must be over the legal drinking age to get drunk and talk to strangers.*

BEAR ON TRAVELLING AND LIFE BUILDING

Aged 19, I made a life-changing decision while I was standing on top of a roof. As I looked out across the tops of those grey, old houses, all of a sudden it was like I'd seen bright sunshine

– I was inspired, and I always say, "Act on inspiration as soon as it strikes." On top of that roof, inspiration struck me big time: I could either use the bit of money I'd saved to rent my own place … or I could use it to go travelling. "Go travelling," I told myself, "definitely." BRILLIANT. I mean, I was single, good-looking, I knew how to talk people around – I could blag myself round the world if I needed to, that's how fucking delightful I am.

I already had £350 in the bank and, because I'm so delightful, my mum bought me a one-way £600 ticket to Hong Kong, then on to Australia. I changed most of my money up into Aussie dollars (the pound was worth having back then) and £50 into Hong Kong dollars. Then my brother Danny put £500 into my bank, and I was a baller.

A couple of my mates came travelling with me, but their parents had given them absolutely loads of money. I often found myself without enough money to buy food, and I knew they had loads in the bank – but did they buy me fish and chips or something? Did they fuck. I remember this one night they all wanted to go out for a meal and asked me to go, even though they knew I was brassic and couldn't even afford to buy a fucking peanut, so off they went without me for their slap-up dinner and left me out. I never forgot that, duly noted. When people are inconsiderate, I think it's a really terrible quality and it can put me off someone very quickly.

Bitter? Me? Nah. I've just got a good memory – partly because I bought a big black notebook and scrapbook from WHSmith,

which I've still got. I started it on the day I left for Hong Kong.
I collected bits from everything I'd been doing in there: tickets,
passes and loads of photos – plus all the stuff that I planned
to do. It was December 2009 then, and still seen as normal
to get your photos printed out. No one does that anymore.
I like to document everything: my thoughts and feelings, where
I've been, how much it cost, and how funny it was – if I could
afford to go. I also put loads of sketches in there; and I wrote
"the world is yours" in there, which is a good reminder.

When I was in Hong Kong, I went on a mountain excursion.
I went all the way to the top and walked round seeing the
crazy sights – like, massive mountains! Speaking of massive,
I also did my first prostitute over there. But actually, it was all
very seedy and weird. I picked a woman with a blue dress on.
I walked all the way up these grotty stairs and there she was,
"Come in, come in," she said. She had all these dirty plates
in the sink, and there was a little mattress in the corner of the
room. She said, "Okay let's go!" I was a bit scared and I said,
all sheepish, "Err … okay?" Then she said, "You got rubber?"
and I said, "Naa, I ain't actually," – because I didn't. So she
gave me one and we did the business. I went out, and, well,
it's haunted me ever since. I was only there for a little while
but still, that was pretty much the highlight of Hong Kong.
I wouldn't recommend it, though …

Three days later, I arrived in Australia and paid up-front for
two weeks in a hostel. I was single the whole time I was in
Australia. Not because I planned it that way, I was just moving
around all the time and there was no point thinking about the

girls I met in terms of relationships. So I just slept around and did what I wanted – especially in hostels. Those places are rife for a quick bunk-up. People also move on all the time – so one night someone is sleeping right next to you, and then you never see them again after the following morning.

When I got there, I didn't know many places – or many people for that matter – so I mooched about quite a lot to begin with. Then, a few days after I arrived, I ended up walking into this bar called Bondi Rocks. I hardly had enough to buy myself a drink – I was struggling so badly at that point – but I met a guy called Stuart Fricker. He could tell how skint I was, but he took a shine to me (you can't blame him). If you ever find yourself down and out in a country you don't know very well, that's the best tip: just get chatting to people in a bar. When they've had a bit of a drink, they're more likely to do you a favour. Be ready to charm them with your amazing personality – this is more important than any qualification you'll ever get at school.

So I smashed Stuart with my charisma, and he kindly said that instead of wasting money at the hostel, I could live with him and his girlfriend Katy for a while. She was from Islington (not far from me) and she had big boobs, brown hair and brown eyes – she was lovely. I don't know if she got fed up with me after the first day, but that might have been the case.

Stuart was a carpenter by trade. He tried to get me a job roofing over there but that didn't go well, so he tried to get me a carpenter job too, but he couldn't find me work doing that either. He carried on trying regardless, and eventually he spoke to this guy called Joe Sweeney who got me a job at Aussie Farmers Direct. They gave me a job working for Wollongong, which is a place in New South Wales that produced the best posh bread, cheese and milk – it was expensive stuff but well worth it. My job was to go door-to-door selling it. How it worked was, seven of us would go on a bus, and you'd have a list of all the produce you had available on the bus, and what you had, you sold. I used to make about 15 sales a day, which was really brilliant, positively legendary. In fact, I ended up being their top salesman and used to get decent bonuses. I'd do the customers good deals too, like "buy twice a week and get a discount". Plus, they loved my banter. I usually did two knocks then wait, then another two knocks. If they had a bell, the same drill. My advice is always give them a big flashy smile when they open the door. It sets you up for a happy time while you are on the doorstep, even if they are miserable.

While I was out in Australia I also had a job fruit picking and loved being outdoors; it was in a little village called Atherton. I ended up holing up with the farmer's daughter. She was lovely. The farmer grew mandarins and limes in his plantation. He was such a nice guy and even though he knew I'd banged his daughter the night before, he still made me a fry-up in the mornings (I actually just wanted to get showered and be left alone). Needless to say, my fruit picking ended pretty swiftly and I left town.

But with my door-to-door food sales, I still had a bit of cash at the end of the trip and I decided it was time to make one more wild journey. Everyone had talked about Thailand but I'd missed out last time, so this time around it had to be done. Off I went for a six-week adventure, and it was just one big party out there – I made the most of every single second. I was in the pool at a party once, and I'd just thrown a girl who had a plaster cast on into the pool (she went mad), when I found a wallet with my foot. Guess what? It had $600 in it. I thought about handing it in to the DJ or the barman, but I knew they would have just nicked it anyway. So I thought, "Do I hand it in and let the barmen have a great time? Or do I use it to treat my friends and have a great couple of weeks?" Of course, I chose to treat my friends to a great couple of weeks. We all had such a brilliant time because of that little find. I didn't have a job in Thailand, but finding that money was such a touch – it helped me enjoy things I wouldn't have been able to do if I hadn't found it: I bought clothes and food for all of us, we hired quad bikes to ride across the beach – I called my bike White Lightening – and Thailand is famous for its moody gear, so I bought a load of great fake clothes including a really nice not-Ralph Lauren for three pounds. I still love that shirt. But most of the time, I just partied.

Probably the most memorable party I went to was the Full Moon party at Ko Pha Ngan – I know it's the one that everyone talks about but it is the event to go and do over there. There's nothing else like it in the world. It's always held on the night before, or the night after, the full moon, and it's basically an all-night beach party and it goes on until the sun rises the following day – but the bars stay open day and night so you can just carry on when daytime arrives. After that, we did Koh

Samui on mopeds; my mates and I just went everywhere on mopeds.

While I was in Thailand I also went to a Tiger temple, which was phenomenal. I respect quiet, serious places like that (probably all that church as a kid).

It was also in Thailand that I got to do my second prostitute. It was me, my mate John and my mate Luke. We'd heard about this place round the corner from our hostel. It had some brick stairs that went up to all these different rooms. So we went round there, up the stairs, and there they all were – lined up against the wall. One in particular took a shine to me and she said, "You get hard, bang bang." Well, you can't argue with that, so "bang bang" it was.

I felt so guilty after that naughty bit of "bang bang", but the guilt only lasted for about three seconds and then I thought, "Nah mate, that was actually amazing."

After that, I went to Cambodia on a coach, and then on to Vietnam – which is where I went to the gun range. I got to shoot the guns they actually used in the Vietnam War, which was a bit cool. I am a wicked shot, as well.

Next, I decided to travel around Bali – I decided just as I was about to get on the plane home. I just thought, "Nah mate, Bali's the one for me, not London ..." so I quickly got all of my luggage off the plane (which the cabin crew were really annoyed about). But then after I'd got all my luggage off of the plane to

London, I suddenly realised that I didn't have enough money to buy a ticket to Bali; so I had to go back to London after all that!

I could have just stayed in Thailand a bit longer. I did think about it, but all good things must come to an end, and I was ready to put some of the great ideas I'd been writing about in my notebook into practice. I'd been travelling a year by this point, and was ready to make a fortune (I did also kind of miss my family, too). So I decided that I'd see the family for a bit, and go back on the roofs while I made my plans, and that's exactly what I did.

Although I'd gone home, I knew this wouldn't be the end of my adventures abroad. I had a taste for travelling and the world was my oyster; but for now I was quite happy to be back home. Then one night while I was watching TV an advert to audition for *The Only Way Is Essex* came on the screen. It said, "People compare Essex to Hollywood. Apply to be on our show …" complete with a limo and shit in the beginning (classy stuff). Everyone was like, "Bear you should apply," and I was like, "Too fucking right." So I went outside to the front of my house and made a video: "Hi, my name is Stephen Bear, I'm 21 and I'm a roofer." Doesn't get better than that really does it?

Thirty people get chosen for *TOWIE*'s audition process, and they just keep getting rid of people until the last person left gets to be on the show. When I auditioned, the rest of the cast for the first season had already been chosen and I was one of the 30 people they ended up selecting for the auditions. We all had to go to Faces nightclub for a speed-dating event to see who was good on camera and who was funny – I was wearing a white t-shirt and a leather jacket, and I'm hilarious, so I pretty much had it in the bag. There were four rounds of auditions and I smashed every single one, and, of course, I ended up winning the whole thing. I remember telling my friends, "I'm gonna be on *TOWIE*!" By that point, everyone in Essex knew who I was – I even remember meeting Kirk Norcross that night, as well as Sam Faiers and Amy Childs.

What happened on the very first episode of the show (ever) was fate: I walked into Visage bar and didn't have a clue what was going on – there were cameras everywhere – but because I was actually supposed to be the main character, I walked in there like I was cock of the walk (which I thought I was), chatting to everyone, being loud and stuff. But I was a bit immature back then and, me being me, I think I rubbed some people up the wrong way. The vibe just got really weird, and all of a sudden it was on me to walk out, so I thought, "Fuck this," and that's exactly what I did. I went walkies.

As I was going home I was thinking, "I don't need this show, it's all bollocks anyway." But my brother Danny went mad at me because it was a big opportunity, which made me think twice about having walked out. So somehow I managed to get my way back on the show in a scene where I was pouring drinks in a club for Mark Wright's birthday. But on the night of filming, even though I was going to be doing stuff in the show, I had to wait outside in the queue. That was when I saw James Argent; he said "hello" and just went straight in while I stood waiting there like a muppet. I thought, "I don't really want to pour drinks that much, fuck this for a laugh." So I went home and on Monday morning, went back on the roofs.

How bad did I feel a few weeks later when TOWIE exploded? It was just everywhere. They were making fortunes and I was filthy-dirty on a roof. I remember watching the stars go into the clubs and my friends telling me, "That could have been you," and it ate me up inside. I was so jealous of Joey Essex. Still, I told myself, "It'll all work out in the end," but I did feel embarrassed for mucking it up.

My next adventure was after I'd been on the show *Shipwrecked* – which I'll tell you about later – and it was time for me to start thinking about getting an agent and that kind of thing. But I'd started to wonder if this showbiz life was for me after all. Basically, I had itchy feet. So I did the sensible thing and went out to Ibiza instead for six months.

It was 2012 and while the Olympics were going on back in London, I was working at Lineker's bar in Ibiza – the White Island. Wayne Lineker – Gary Lineker's brother – is the owner there. Apparently, he and his brother used to get along well enough, but they were worlds apart in the things that floated their individual boats. Obviously, Gary was known for being one of England's best ever football players, but the more famous he became in sport and TV, the more Wayne seemed to party

– maybe it was to make him feel a bit better for not being able to play for England himself. Shame.

As well as Lineker's, Wayne owned a place called Ocean Beach, which is a massive bar and club. It's a beautiful place to work, I have to say. At Ocean Beach all the action is focused around a massive swimming pool. They throw these "bed days" where everyone just sits back, chills, and listens to Balearic tunes and chilled-out house music. Sometimes they have famous people come and do a live set there, other times it's just famous people getting pissed there.

When I was working with them as a barman, I thought I was like Tom Cruise in that film *Cocktail*. I loved it because I was the centre of attention. But one day, not really thinking it was so bad, I got caught out for being naughty: I'd be given money for drinks and not put it through the tills. I mean come on, everyone does it – just maybe I was doing it a bit more than others. After a while, though, everyone began wondering why I had so much money for drinks and food, and why I was always treating them all to stuff. Then my best mate grassed me up and told Wayne I was doing some naughty things that I shouldn't be doing. So I walked in there, wearing my little red shorts, completely oblivious that I'd been grassed up, all happy and smiling like the Mr Number One Barman I was, and said "Hey Wayne, what's happening?" He said to me, "I know what you've been up to, you've been stealing." Busted. I politely told him "Well, I wouldn't exactly call it stealing, Wayne – I need to pay for my rent and to live." I even told him that I probably deserved a slap, but he didn't. He just told me that I had to leave the island (yeah, no biggy). After a week, I managed to give him back €200 through my friend James; but he still wanted me off the island – everyone was looking for me, saying I was going to get my legs broken. But no one scares me, I don't leave anywhere – and broken legs would only make it harder for me to do so (idiot). So I stayed (and I hid). Then the next year, I went back and did the same season for six months, just to wind him up.

Funny thing is, after all this time, he's ended up unblocking me on Twitter – that's how fame hungry he is. I think my ex, Vicky Pattison, had something to do with him unblocking me because one night, while we were together, he suddenly messaged her saying, "If you're coming to Ibiza soon, make sure you come to my bar, Ocean Club." So she said back to him, "Er, I don't think you like my boyfriend very much, though …" He of course knew that I was seeing her, so he told her, "As long as he apologises, he can come back in." Well, I don't apologise to anyone. He should have just laughed it off, not threatened to break my legs. I mean, what's all that about? We're not in fucking Goodfellas. Not to mention the fact that I made it up to him by paying all his money back, admitting I'd done wrong.

When I lived out in Ibiza, I also threw some amazing boat parties – and I tell you what, they were terrific. I called them "Dirty Funk" and got that boat rocking. I knew everyone on that island and I've still got friends that I made out there. Ibiza, for me, is the BEST place in the world, no question. I know it inside out, I even wanted to open a bar in Ibiza – it was part of my business plan for the future – and I definitely want to have a home out there one day.

It's probably a little bit rude, but I still think one of my all-time favourite nights from my time in Ibiza was when I was out one night in San Antonio and I think someone must've spiked my drink because I took a bird back to mine, and I don't know how it started, but I ended up licking her bum for about four hours (she was clean, though, as she'd had a shower first). I told her to get on all fours and woof like a dog, so she did … for about four hours, pretending to be a dog. Howling, barking, the lot. Then I came to, and thought, "What the fuck am I doing?" She was probably wondering the same thing because we laughed about it the next day when we saw each other.

One of my funniest travelling stories was when I was on one of my first boys holidays in Zante, Greece. It was 2008, and a massive group of us had gone out there. I did nutty things most nights while I was with that group. This story's a bit different, though, because I was totally alone when it happened, and I have not got a clue what was going through my head. One night, I was out with the group, but I had got so fucking drunk that when I walked around to try and find them I couldn't see anyone I knew. So I started slowly walking back to my hotel along the main the strip (and stopped for a few more shots on the way). It was just a leisurely stroll back really; I knew where my hotel was so it should've been no problem. I wasn't worried about it; but then I did start to think I might not actually know where my hotel was after all. I kept walking a bit longer anyway because I was having a lovely little time, then all of a sudden I realised I didn't have a clue where I was.

In hindsight, I should have just turned around and retraced my steps, but I didn't think about turning back or asking for directions, oh no. I did what anyone (that drunk) would do it the same situation … that's right, my best idea was to take all of my clothes off and dive into a nearby bush. My next amazing idea was to spend the entire night there, so I fell asleep in the nude in the bush. I don't know why I did it, I really don't – it was without a doubt a fucking weird thing to do. I don't even know how long I spent in the bush but I woke up, and it was light. I tried to remember about where I'd been, or what I'd been doing; but there was no explanation at all for my decision. After a few seconds of standing there, I thought, "Where are my clothes?" Turns out my clothes had been stolen – who nicks the clothes from a naked man in a bush? "This is not good," I thought. I mean, I was naked, so I had to just find my way back to my hotel with no clothes on (I made a lot friends, and a lot of enemies on the way). I got back to the room and told the boys, "You'll never guess what happened to me last night – I took all my clothes off and got into a bush!" But nobody batted an eyelid.

Some people might say that I should have had my fill of travelling; but honestly, I've got so many more places to see – I'm not going to stop now! I definitely need to spend some time in Hollywood, and I'd like to do Vegas next year too. There's a lot more journeys left in me, let's just wait and see where I spontaneously end up next.

BEARZY'S TOP TIPS FOR TRAVELLING AND LIFE BUILDING

Having some extra cash made a huge difference to how much I enjoyed my travels; so I'd recommend trying to get a job (or stealing a wallet) if you're travelling for a while. For example, door-to-door sales is paid well and is hardly rocket science – confidence is the key to success in that game. You've just got to believe that you're the best salesman in the world and that you're impossible to say no to (so kind of like a night out). If you believe that you're the best at something, that belief eventually rubs off on you, stays with you, and other people start to believe it. There's no such thing as too confident when you're selling (especially when you're trying to get rid of cheese in 40 degree heat) – make eye-contact, and most of all, be likeable and memorable.

If you're on your own, you don't always have someone to watch your back, and sometimes you get yourself in situations where some idiot wants to fuck you over – that rarely happens in Australia as the people are so cool, but needless to say it does still happen. However, the saying "safety in numbers" isn't necessarily true either – I always found it easier to meet people and have fun on my own. And sometimes it's just knowing the difference between good vibes and bad vibes in a different country. If you get into a cab, for example, find out first how long it takes, and how much it costs to get to and from wherever you are going – this is so you don't get ripped off for a fucking fortune and end up with no money for "bang bang"! When you are travelling around on your own, you are more likely to be taken for a ride (in both senses of the word), so ask the taxi driver for a rough estimate of the fare before you leave. If it's way off what someone else is saying (ask a couple of taxi drivers if you can be arsed), or from what you know to be true, take a different cab and tell that driver he's being a cunt. You might get punched, you might get run over, but it'll be worth it: you can get an ambulance to take you to where you're going.

Another benefit of knocking around alone is that your mistakes are your own, and your wins are your own – so it's way more exciting. There's no worrying that your decision to go waterskiing at midnight is going to fuck someone off, or that throwing a BBQ in your kitchen might annoy someone. Want to go back to the bar you were in last night and bang the waitress?

Do it. Want to go shopping for some vegetables at the market that you have never seen before? Do it. Want to sleep in all day? Do it! Because you are on your own, so who cares? Do you? No? Then great, let's party. It's your own day to do what you like – make it educational for yourself too, mind.

In Australia they call everyone "mate," whether they know you or not – do not, however, assume that being called "mate" means they like you. If the "aaaa" starts lasting a bit longer, they actually fucking love you. But if it's a short, sharp "mate", they're probably about to knock you the fuck out, and you need to run. Also, Aussies do like to take the piss out of each other, but tourists especially. So don't be offended if they start ripping the shit out of you about your flip-flops – oh and they call flip-flops "thongs" in Australia, which is a bit kinky. Anyway, apparently if they take the piss out of you it's because they actually like you. It's a strange old thing.

If you're not sure what to take on your travels, it's simple: don't take too much. For one, don't take a sleeping bag unless you're actually going camping. They're useless. Most hostels won't even let you use them, although I've got no idea why, it's just another of life's little mysteries. Make sure that you don't pack too many clothes either. Remember: you'll buy things while you travel and you'll be sorry you don't have room to get that moody Ralph Lauren stuff. You only really need to take two pairs of shoes and two pairs of trousers. Just make sure you've got enough Calvin Kleins – they're the most important thing, just them and your passport really and you're good to go. But do take soap because most hostels don't have any – or if they do it's proper scummy and covered in pubes, and it's nice to have one covered in your own pubes. Don't bother taking pills for medicine with you either. All you need is the sunshine to make you feel better – trust me, I'm a celebrity. And if you cut your leg, just wash it in the sea because salt water is the best thing for you ever ... although you might attract a shark so you want to watch that. And on that note, don't go in too deep.

Also you have to avoid temptation with those travel shops, because you can just go mad buying novelty hats and plastic shit because it's funny, and it is. But you can spend so much cash just buying money belts, karabiners and hiking shoes that you'll (hopefully) never end up wearing. Only have clothes you know you'll always wear – and just so you know, using a money belt is like carrying around a sign saying "Whack me over the head and rob me now. Please."

I was mugged only recently and it was shit. But I wasn't that bothered because he didn't get away with my mobile phone and all my contacts – that would have been a fucking nightmare. What happened was, one moment he was talking to me as I was standing by my car, asking me if I lived locally and being all nice and polite – I thought he was just a fan. All of a sudden, he just fucking punched me, knocked me on the floor and started battering my head. Then he pulled my watch off of me, which was a fake rose-gold Hublet. I mean, it was a lovely looking watch but worth nothing because it was moody. I shouted to him, "It's a fake mate, you can fucking have it," but he obviously didn't believe me. He took my wallet with my bank cards in it, and as I got up to have a pop at him, he ran away. It's with things like this that you have to think, "Is it honestly worth getting knifed over?" I don't think so. And the funny thing is, if anyone had wanted my watch (and bothered to ask me) I'd have said, "Here it is mate, you can have it," because that's what I'm like.

But back to travelling, these are my most practical tips:

Know about plug sockets. The Australian one's aren't British ones, as you might expect because you're not in Britain any more. But the people speak English, so, if you're like me, you'd think the plugs must be English too. But they're not – neither are the American or European ones. The Australian ones are basically the American ones, but drunkenly sloping inwards.

The best way to cure a hangover? Get up early and seize the day. By the time you've noshed down a greasy breakfast and found yourself in the next place, the hangover is totally forgotten about. Until you go out that night and wake up with another one the following morning – groundhog day. In hostels, you will meet a whole new group of friends on each of your journeys. Never be afraid to say goodbye to do your own thing because, chances are, their idea of a good time and your ideas might be very, very different.

I think my last tip would be: don't judge other people's lifestyles if they're different from your own. Listen to opinions you don't agree with and disagree if you like, but listen first to what their way of doing things is. Different doesn't mean wrong, does it?

Embrace different possibilities or suggestions people might have – you might end up have a blinding time because of an idea that someone else told you about. Ask questions, just like in my school tips. You don't have to agree, but you may be surprised what you learn.

Ultimately, inspiration was all it took for me to go travelling, sheer genius imagination – if you don't act on the things that inspire you in life, you won't get anywhere. People get an idea and it's brilliant, but they forget about it because they're too scared to act on it. Scared of what, though? Scared of getting it wrong, that's what; but getting it wrong's part of the fun of it.

I've always had so many ideas, and I've never been in a position to execute them before because I've had no money. But now, I'm in a position to do my own bits and bobs as I'm earning more. For example, my first idea is my clothing line East End Clobber. People often think I'm silly and that I'll go off the rails; but what people will see in time is that I'm a doer.

My girlfriends have also inspired me to do well. Vicky was so clever and Lillie had her own clothing line. I'm good at picking girlfriends – I like clever girls that you can learn from.

So basically, my top tips for travelling are: get a good idea, or a good girlfriend, and get inspired! Just follow your heart, try and get a job, get chatting to people, don't get your drink spiked, try not to steal from the till – basically don't do a lot of the things I did – and you'll be fine.

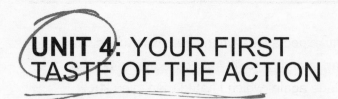

UNIT 4: YOUR FIRST TASTE OF THE ACTION

This chapter gives a general overview of the Shipwrecked experience and how Bear got to be on the show. It also reveals Bear's feelings towards the rest of the Shipwrecked cast, and how the adventure to a faraway island can change your perspective on life ... for a couple of days, anyway.

The chapter concludes with a consolidation of Bear's most prized tips on how to get on the show, from audition techniques to why you should hide your fear and believe in yourself.

Students will be tested on this, at some point in their lives.

BEAR ON HIS FIRST SHOW

I was so gutted after fucking things up with *TOWIE*, gutted.

I was brooding over it every single day and my whole family knew it – they couldn't avoid it! I was just moping round the house for months. Then, around six months later, Danny said to me, "Channel 4 are auditioning for *Shipwrecked*, you should apply." I thought I had no chance – it's only friends of friends that ever get onto shows like that. But Danny said that I was being a "massive div" and, "All you have to do is fill out a form online." Now, I hate forms, I'll do anything to avoid filling them in; but because I was still feeling a bit sore about the *TOWIE* thing, I made myself do it. I wasn't prepared to look like a mug again for missing out.

I didn't have any expectations when I sat down and did it, but soon I got an interview for it! I got called up to London, and I had to queue again, which I hated (don't you know who I am?). So I said to one of the TV guys, "Do I really have to queue up for all this? Just stick me on the island," and he started to laugh. When I (finally) got to the front of the queue and got inside, I did this three-minute "speed round"; and then after that they sent me through to the next round. When I walked into the next round it was in a small room and a bit awkward, but I got them laughing straightaway by saying, "What is this, an orgy?" to the runner and the cameraman. Then I showed them the bear tattoo I've got on my tummy, and I told them, "Yeah man, I'm the Bear." I had all of their attention and I knew that I'd stick in their memory.

I was right, because the next meeting I had was with Kate Bates – she's one of the producers on the show. I sat down and she said, "Clear your diary … you're going away for the summer." And that was it, I'd got in. I couldn't believe my luck, so I kept thinking to myself, "I'm not going to mess this up, I'm going to stick it out and make the most of every second in Fiji. I'll be funny, but I'll be sensible. But my main goal is that everyone remembers me; I'm not going to fade away into the background with this, I'm going to cause controversy." And that's where the telly version of Stephen Bear really started. So I packed my trunks and some clean pants, then off I went to meet the rest of the islanders.

Basically, how *Shipwrecked* works is: each week, they vote someone into power, and the person who ends up with the most red beads wins it. I know I could have won, but I was naughty twice and had a bead taken off of me (bastards). The first naughty incident was when I stole a lighter; I thought it would be handy to start a fire with. And the other time was when they said you couldn't swim across to see the others; well, I decided to do it so I could see Anna – obviously wish I hadn't now.

Speaking of which, I'd sum up the *Shipwrecked* castaways like this:

Anna: What a bitch. I started going out with her and I actually really liked her; but as far as she was concerned, I wasn't good enough for her. I was so skint but I bought her a rose gold bracelet with all the money I had in the world and, after that, she left me for someone else.

Tristan: Really liked him, he made me laugh.

Brimes: Top geezer, loved that guy.

Dominique: She was a really nice, down-to-earth girl who got my banter – and not all girls do, because not all girls are cool.

Joe: What a fucking dick he was.

Kitten: She was a right idiot. She didn't get my humour and started to hate on me, trying to make everyone else join in. She was ruthless.

I think it really helped that I'd done some travelling before I went on the island, because I'd had to put up with people in those sorts of situations already – like noisy twats in hostels when you're trying to sleep, you just throw a pillow at their head and they stop snoring. No arguments there. I'd also slept on a beach before because I'd had no money – one morning I woke up next to a tramp, clutching my bag. But I knew all these things would serve me well in *Shipwrecked.*

Shipwrecked felt like a dream: I was trapped on an island with nothing but sea around me – no phone, nothing. I started to contemplate life there too, "What is life?" I'd think to myself. "What am I doing here? There must be a reason why we're all here." It was deep shit, and my outlook on life totally changed during that period on the island. There were kids playing with balls made out of bits of rag and they were happy with what they had; it gave me such perspective on life. Back home, we had free healthcare, everything we could ever need – yet we all still moaned. It didn't seem right. It's always made me feel lucky ever since. I did have the most fucked-up dreams when I came home, though. It takes ages to get back to normal.

By the time I came back it was January 2015 and freezing cold on the roof of a house. But all those thoughts and visions were still with me; and people had started to know who I was. Certainly the Essex lot knew who I was – I'd get straight to the front of the queue at clubs. I know it's a bit of a mug-y thing to do, but who wants to wait in the cold? I don't. I felt like I'd completed life after *Shipwrecked*, and I didn't have time to freeze my balls off anymore.

BEARZY'S TOP TIPS FOR GETTING ON YOUR FIRST SHOW

Now the thing about *Shipwrecked* is this: not only
do they want big characters, they also want people
who are fearless – and I mean scared of *nothing*.
Remember, you're going to be stuck on an island in
the middle of nowhere for a month and you can't be
someone who is going to piss their pants on day one
– this is Rambo shit. So you've got to come across
in your audition like you've had a crack at this life –
you've had the lightening bolts it throws at you, but
you've come through it all and survived. If you're lucky
and haven't had life challenge you much, come across
as invincible anyway – it's the same as being a salesman,
just believe in yourself.

You can't have wimpy characters on a show like
Shipwrecked, they aren't going to build a hut, make a
fire or skin an animal, and that's what the show is all
about. Me, I'd skin a tortoise if I needed to – I don't
care that tortoises have a hard shell and no skin, I'll
skin 'em anyway – and the TV producers got that from
me the first time they saw me. If you are scared in
the audition or at any point, hide it and work on that
problem later. Make sure you come across as someone

who wants a challenge, loves life; but who also loves adding a bit of drama in the mix, too. It's a winning combo for *Shipwrecked.* Oh, and turn up with a tan so they know you'll look good on telly, I reckon that also helps.

Shipwrecked is one of the original reality TV programmes and it set me up for life, for which I am truly grateful. Would I go back to a desert island now and live there for a month? Of course I would … it's an adventure and you don't want to ever miss out on that.

UNIT 5: EX ON THE BEACH

You will be taught about Bear's first and second experiences on Ex On The Beach in this chapter; including why he decided to take part, how a shepherd's pie his mum cooked nearly got in the way of him applying and his thoughts on the cast of both series.

The chapter will also detail how to get on Ex On The Beach (by going out with a lot of people), how to behave in auditions and why you shouldn't be scared of revealing the skeletons in your closet.

Please note: If they do not have their own skeletons, students should not remove any skeletons from the science lab to fill their closets.

BEAR ON EX ON THE BEACH 1

So it's January 2015, and there I am, back home again, standing on a roof, freezing my nuts off. At this point in time, all of my friends were telling me that I'd never make any of the plans that I had told them about happen. "You'll see," I told them. "I may take my time about things, but I'll get there. No dramas," I thought. I knew that one day I'd prove them all wrong, and then they'd have to eat their words.

Then one day, after a long slog on the roofs, I checked my Twitter and noticed a production company called Whizz Kid had started following me. If you don't know much about how television shows are made: a production company, or a production house, is the company responsible for making the show itself, as opposed to the channel that it goes on. The production company is also responsible for getting all the funding to make the show, and for paying the people on it – so in a way, all new shows are a big risk and depend on the fact that the channels are interested enough in the show being made for the production company to put their money into making it. Basically, the production company does all of the making of the show, and then the channel buys it and puts it on air.

So, as for the production company in this case, Whizz Kid, they'd obviously tracked me down on social media and I decided to follow them back. It said on their page that they worked for MTV. I was seeing a bird on-and-off called Connie, who worked with Cirque le Soir, at the time, and they'd interviewed her for the show *Ex On The Beach*. She'd obviously mentioned me as someone she'd been going out with – and they'd started doing their research on me. They messaged me, asking me if I felt like going away to a hot location with the possibility of becoming MTV's next big reality star. Well, I was still shivering after all those hours on the roof so a bit of sunshine and success sounded right up my street (plus, I love seeing myself on telly – looking at myself on screen is well cool). But, it would mean another form to fill in – absolute nightmare! Just as I was about to start the form, my mum came in with my dinner; it was shepherd's pie. I thought about doing the form, then I thought, "Nah. Fuck this, I want my dinner." So, I ate my shepherd's pie (it was banging) but the whole time I was munching, the form was running through my head, it wouldn't stop. So I thought, "I've got to just do it." And I did; after I'd finished the pie. The production company wanted a recent picture of me, so I stuck two beauties at the top of the form, filled it in and sent it off.

I waited patiently, but over the next few nights my mind wandered when I lay in bed and I started to feel anxious, thinking maybe I'd made a massive fuck-up on the form. But the next thing I knew, I'd got an interview and as we know, I smash it in any interview – everyone loves me – so it's no surprise I went in there and sailed through the chat with them – I was the P&O Ferries of chat.

But the interview process I had to go through was a long one, with loads and loads of questions from Sophie and Jack from Whizz Kid. They must have been scouring about, trying to find out what they could – and they'd no doubt watched *Shipwrecked,* which would have given them a good idea of what I was about. I told them all about what I'd been up to and why they needed me for that new series in Mexico.

It turned out that they liked me better than Connie, even though she was the one that got me in there (told you I picked good girlfriends). They thought I was so amazing that they suggested I should be one of the *Ex On The Beach* originals, and that she'd be one of the exes. Bad luck Connie, but I was right in there. She came on the last episode absolutely fuming, which was a bit shit. But overall I met some cool people during my time there, including Megan McKenna. She'd already been on *TOWIE* at that point in the girl band Lola with Jess Wright. I like Megan; I like it that she's doing well. She told me "well done" when I won *Big Brother*, but she's not interested in plugging my clothing line as a favour – so when I'm writing the final scene at the end of my film, she's not going to be in it. She was also mates with Connie, but that didn't last long because Connie shagged Megan's boyfriend Harry when they were still together – yeah, whoopsy.

When I got back from *Ex On The Beach*, I did what I always do: I went back to roofing for a while. It was weird because being away in Mexico didn't even seem real, it didn't feel like it had happened. Probably partly because the show hadn't come on yet; and there I was back doing what I always do like nothing had changed. Roofing is in my blood, though. I think, no matter where I end up, it'll always be a part of who I am.

I'm sure you're gagging to know, so here's my thoughts on the *EOTB* 1 lot:

Griff: Absolutely HATED him. When everyone was shouting at me, he'd join in just for the sake of it when I'd done nothing to him.

Megan: Love Megan. Who doesn't? She's gorgeous and fiery and, she's just Megan. She's done so well in the last year, and fair play to her.

Tristan: Loved him, he was so funny. I got him, he got me. He's the kind of fella you don't mind being away with for a month at all.

Cami: Hated her. What a bitch. She was alright to me on the show but the tables soon turned when we got home. When I was going out with Vicky, she said all kinds of things to her that weren't true. She decided to slate me for absolutely no reason and caused me endless and needless agg.

Kirk: Liked him a lot. A lot of people don't like him, but I like those people that no-one else gets.

Jayden: Love that guy, he's something else. I still can't work him out, but I don't think anyone can. He is on another planet. What a strange cat.

Holly: Loved her, she's cool. One of the good girls, easy to be around and took everything in her stride – like that in a girl.

Ali: Loved her too. Most of the girls there were great to be fair, except Cami (the bitch).

When I got back, I was asked to go back on **TOWIE** again. I couldn't believe it! That had been my biggest regret before I left. But now, I was better than that. Much better. Mark Wright? Mark WHO mate.

BEAR ON EX ON THE BEACH 2

Ex On The Beach had changed everything for me – I felt like people were getting what I was actually about for the first time in my life. I also ended up doing a lot of personal appearances off the back of it, which was amazing. But I spent all the money I earned pretty quickly … so I went back to trusty old roofing (when I say it changed "everything" for me, it didn't change that).

Then, out of the blue, I got the call from Whizz Kid (who make *Ex On The Beach*, remember) asking if I wanted to do the next series. Of course I wanted to do the next series – are you mental? Better still, this series was in Thailand – which of course I knew well from travelling – so I also knew that I would 100 per cent smash it over there. I was going to be one of the "originals" on the show again, and I was pretty sure I knew which of my exes was going to arrive, and I was pretty sure it would be dynamite. So off I went to Thailand …

The second time round I was a lot more confident, mainly because I knew what was going on this time. I'd learnt from the first series what would make the final edit, and had become an expert on how to be the star of the show. All I had to do was put the producers' brains into my head (not literally, that's more *Dexter*) and give them what they want. With reality TV, I think this really is the trick: always think, "what do they want, what would make great storylines, what would they love from me? How can I make myself stand out this time, but in a different way?" Ultimately, I knew the best way to make the show all about me was by ramping up the drama. And yes, of course that meant making things kick off when they probably wouldn't have done otherwise.

I started this *EOTB* adventure in classic Bear style: when I first got there I had a chaperone looking after me, but just before we started filming, my chaperon had the day off and I was left to my own devices. The TV crew had told me that I couldn't leave the premises, so I decided to make it look like I hadn't left the premises. I put pillows underneath the bed covers so it looked like I was actually in bed – genius. I'd seen the trick in a film when a kid sneaks out to a party, and guess what? When I snuck out and they came to check on me, they thought I was asleep. Kids have all the best ideas. I wandered around and came across a party in Ko Samui. Ko Samui is the second largest island in Thailand and has a massive tourist population, as well as 24-hour bars everywhere (which must just be a coincidence). So that night, to connect with the locals, I got extremely drunk.

I was hoping to go to this Buffalo Fighting Festival I'd heard the island was known for, but I couldn't find it, so I wound up going to this amazing club full of girls. After a few minutes I thought, "Hang on a second, all these birds look the same … but who cares, they're pretty fit." So I bought a drink and got chatting to one of them. It was all going well, until I saw his/her Adam's apple and I realised that, actually, all the "girls" in this club weren't girls, they were ladyboys. I pulled this fit bird who I thought might still be a girl anyway, chatted her up like normal, "Alright babe, how are you?" all that stuff. She said, "Oh good, you want bang bang?" I thought, "Yeah, actually babe, funny

coincidence, I do." It all seemed a little bit easy. But still, I went on the back of her moped to a hotel room and got straight down to business and started snogging her. As I got more in the mood, I slowly started moving my hand down and … I found a willy! I was quite shocked. So I stopped the hanky-panky and said, "You know what mate, here's 500 Baht – just give me a blow job." So when the he-she with a nice pair of tits tried to take her jeans off, I just told her I'd rather she kept them on – she did, and that was great. "Here's your money, love," I said, and got a cab back to the hotel like a player. I'll be honest, it was one of the best blowjobs I ever had. Would I do that again? Would a pig eat shit? (Fuck yeah it would.)

A few days after the ladyboy episode, I went to the gym to make sure I looked amazing on the beach in the show. While I was working out, I looked out the window and saw a sign outside that said "massage". There was also a lady outside with a great big pair of tits, so I started getting a semi pretty much straight away. "Sod the workout," I thought, and decided to see what was happening over there instead. I went over all casual, but I didn't really know what to say so I asked this lady where the beach was – lame I know, but what else was I going to say when I wasn't sure if it was a knocking shop or not?

Anyway, she told me where the beach was and then gave me a little look. I just thought, "Fuck it," and said, "How much for a wank?" – doing the hand motion. She smiled at me and said, "Ah! 500 Baht." That sounded pretty good to me, but then she pointed at her mate, saying she was the one who was going to do it. I don't want to be mean, but the other one was so fucking ugly, I just couldn't face it – not even with my eyes closed. So I told her, "Fuck that, I want you, old big tits." I think secretly she was pleased I liked her better because she ended up taking me upstairs. We went into this room with a thin little mattress – same drill as last time – and I asked her, "How much for a blowjob?" She told me it was 800 Baht. I thought, "All good then," and got my shorts off. It was all going well, I was feeling fine and loving life, thinking I was only getting a blowjob, but then she went a bit leftfield. She told me to roll on my back, then she told me to lift up my knees, so I did, and she started licking my arsehole. It wasn't what I was expecting at all, but luckily, I'd showered after the gym. And as it turns out, I love my arsehole being licked, so this was a bonus to say the least. Once she'd had a good old lick, she finished me off and I tried to stand up, but my legs were still shaking. When I did eventually get up, she tried to hug me, and I had to be like, "Nah, you're alright love." So I gave her the 800 Baht, a tip of my hat, and left.

After the rim-job it was finally time to start filming, and I was excited. I was ready for my first bit of action, so when the cameras started rolling, I was straight into the zone of making the show MINE: "Why am I back? Every beach needs a Bear. I'm still waiting to find Goldilocks to jump in my bed and have a little roll around. That's how the story goes, isn't it? On a beach?"

Everyone knew that, as usual, I'd cause everyone agg to get attention – on *EOTB*, it's all about getting attention, because attention leads to dates (classic peacocking). Getting on dates on *EOTB* is THE name of the game. You've got to think about how the producer thinks on this kind of thing: they want you acting up and being full of yourself! No doubt. It's one of those shows where if you think about it a bit beforehand, you can play it perfectly (but never think too much or you won't do enough crazy shit).

You've got a month there, so what you've got to do is pick one girl every three or four days, obviously that you fancy, or at least quite fancy. If you want to blow your load before the show has really started, the worst thing you can do is kiss all the girls on the first day. It's all strategic, plan which girls you want to get with, and spread those snogs out cleverly. How you do that is: pick one, say you like them, then when someone else comes in, you say, "Oh, sorry darling – she's caught my eye now and I am single, after all. Laters!" It might sound a bit tight; but that new girl right there is another storyline, and then I'm the focus of the whole episode again. Boom. That's how magic is done.

My ex on the second series was Kayleigh – but she was more of a one-night stand than an ex. She did a story on me during *Big Brother*, so I think she's a bit of a wrong 'un now anyway. Another ex on the show was Holly Rickward, who I fingered once – apparently, a cheeky finger is the same as cats, a mortgage, the works when it comes to reality telly. On the island, as Kayleigh came out of the sea, I was scared, but I also had a semi. Scared because of who it was going to be, and a semi because of what was coming out of the sea – whoever she was.

But ultimately, it was quite boring with Kayleigh really, so I focused on who I wanted to get with next. Obviously, it was in this series that I met Lillie Gregg, who ended up being the ex that confronted me on *Celebrity Big Brother*. But when she came out of the sea she was Gaz Beadle's ex, and I thought she was gorgeous. She seemed like such a princess, I just wanted to be with her. I also kissed Krysten, Olivia and Amy – just to make sure I got myself on every single episode – but I waited until Lillie and I got a date to put it on her. I liked her a lot. She was lovely, and she was clever. Like I said, I'm always attracted to clever girls – I learn a lot from them. Lillie has her own clothing line back home in Birmingham and did loads of cool stuff with her business; so every day, I learned a little more from her and listened to how she'd made her company work.

After we came back home, Lillie ended up being my girlfriend for four months. We went to Portugal and had some great times going out together. We were always on each other's Snapchats and stuff, we were seen out at events together – clearly smitten with each other. It was a brilliant time for us both, no regrets at all. But ultimately, she wasn't the girl for me and I'd known it from early on. I sort of tried to break it off with her before I went in to the *CBB* house, but I didn't manage to; that left me in quite a difficult situation when it came to the show. And then what happened on the show, happened (unlike Vegas, unfortunately it doesn't stay there).

It was weird that the second series of *EOTB* (when me and Lillie got together) was due to come out after *CBB* had been on, which was when I'd already split up with her. I should have split up with her before the *CBB* house, no doubt about that ... but I did try to. No hard feelings between her and me, though, I'm sure I'll see her out and about one day and have a drink. It's just sometimes in life, you meet someone lovely and it's not even anything particular about them, nothing you can actually put your finger on, you just know that they aren't the right person for you. You can try to force the relationship and try to make it work, but if the spark isn't there, you'll never be able to light a decent fire.

But as far as *EOTB* was concerned, I had smashed it second time round, and word got out that in the new series I was the man to watch – again. That's how I ended up getting the call for *Celebrity Big Brother* – the show that changed everything for me.

My thoughts on the *EOTB 2* cast:

Gaz: Honestly, I love the guy. I got on with him the most because we are on the same level. He just gets it, and he's really funny. As a person, I respect the fact that he's done well and is getting on with it.

Ashley: I used to like him and I got on with him on the show, but now ... not so much.

Hawley: Brilliant fella, there's nothing not to like about Hawley. I really got on with him, top lad.

Conor: I didn't like him. I thought he was a grass in there, and he comes across as being very false everywhere. He's bitchy too. I can't stand blokes like that who try and be your mate and then they are all snaky behind your back. Not a good look.

Kayleigh: I hated her in the end. I know we'd got on alright before the show, but I never really saw a genuinely nice side to her then, and I definitely don't see any niceness in her now. She slagged me off, and wanted Lillie to be with Gaz over me; even though nothing had even happened between me and Lillie at that point – and Gaz had already cheated on Lillie. I mean, that's how much she didn't like me from the start. Kayleigh's got a problem, man.

Lillie: Of course Lillie is a great girl, but she is blatantly still in love with Gaz. I obviously liked her a lot and we were together for those few months, but Lillie is only worried about what she looks like in the press and I was right about her in the end. I see her for what she is now. She likes to play the victim and she went off with someone else and lied about it – but I don't need the agg of going into that.

Jemma: I got on really well with Jemma. We were great mates on both series, but she was best mates with Vicky at the time. Vicky would slag her off to me, and it ended up being in a weird triangle thing. Vicky wouldn't even let her have a picture with me as a mate – a control freak, Vicky is. She wants to have a hold over everyone.

Jemma and Vicky don't talk now …

BEARZY'S TOP TIPS FOR BAGGING A PLACE ON EOTB

Well, I'm not being rude here but there's one trait you need for *EOTB* to get you even to the first hurdle: whether you are a boy or a girl, you need to have been a bit of a shagger in your time, because guess what? They need you to have exes that are alive and well, and who you are willing to tell the producers all about – even if you cheated on them (if they manage to get it out of you).

I was never nervous, but with ex girlfriends I suppose you can't help but feel a little bit anxious about what they might say about you. I always treat women properly, though, so I know I've never had a legitimate worry on that front. Basically, never call them a slag and always be nice to them – it's easy. I'm like that about ex girlfriends anyway, I never say anything bad; it's disrespectful and it's not clever. If you slag off one person to someone, they'll end up thinking, "Bet he does the same to me," – so just don't do it.

Now, I've had quite a few cuddles in my life with a lot of different ladies (and ladyboys) so I could give them a shopping list of girls that I'd seen at one time or another. This is the key thing: don't be scared of your past if you want to go on this show, because it's a programme that's designed to get the skeletons out of your closet, or out of the sea in my case. So if you genuinely never want to see some of your exes again – maybe because you set fire to their mum ... or worse, had sex with their mum, on fire – this is not the show for you.

The other thing about getting into *EOTB* is you have to show the casting guys that you aren't scared of trying it on with another fella's bird, right in front of him. I've never been (much of) one to do this while I'm out, but when it came to the show, you have to put moves on a girl your mate might still be in love with – so if you couldn't do that to someone you like, you're not going to get the airtime. To get that across, you've got to be a bit snidey in your interview – but not so much that they hate you – just enough for them to think, "Yeah, he'd snog a girl every two days to get on telly." That's why I was the ideal cast member.

But the most important thing to remember is: don't even think of turning up to a show like this if you are not B.U.F.F. I've been ripped both times I've been on the show, and there's just no chance that they'd ever pick a fella with a flabby belly to go on. So, to prepare, you have to imagine that you look like one of the last cast members, just visualise what you need to look like and make it happen with a positive mental attitude – don't bother going down the gym, thinking's hard enough.

The audition process for *EOTB* varies a little bit from show to show, but not much. You need to be polite to the producers at all costs; it's very important – little things like putting your phone away and maintaining eye contact. You need to make them laugh, so pack your banter – even if you say something like, "Look mate, if you get me on this show, I'll give you a few hundred quid," and they start to laugh, it's a little icebreaker. But also, you never know… they might fancy a few quid in their back pocket to go out that night and take you up on the offer. In which case, pack some counterfeits – might get you on the show, might get you in jail. Either way it'll be something to do.

Anyway, if they like you as a person, they will always remember you. If you seem relaxed and on their level, they will always put you forward. It's not what you know, it's who you know – it doesn't even matter if you don't actually know them, just act like you do; swagger says it all.

UNIT 6: STYLE

This chapter is as you might expect: an overview and insight into Bear's classic and timeless style. From statement Hawaiian shirts and shaved eyebrows, to blue hair and painted nails, Bear explains exactly why he is so experimental, and gives students tips on how to experiment with their own style. You will also be educated about his tattoos and a bit of Greek mythology.

This chapter will detail which shirts are cool, which shirts are not, how big your t-shirts should be, why it's okay to a buy a bit of "moody" merchandise once in a while, and how Bear's impeccable style has spurred him to launch his own clothing line, East End Clobber.

Students will be tested on which countries it is legal to buy "moody" merchandise in (not the UK). They are also encouraged to get a new haircut as homework. Shaved eyebrows should be reserved for the bravest students only.

BEAR ON STYLE

My style is my style, simple as that. It does change daily: one day I might have a nice bit of nail varnish on, another I'll go for a Hawaiian shirt. I'm just always waking up thinking, "I'll try something new today." It's good to be impulsive; I like to surprise myself. Like one morning I woke up and surprised myself with a shaved eyebrow. Now I like to put one or two lines in there and it's ended up being one of my favourite looks at the moment. I'm going to bring back 1990, whether people like it or not.

I'm probably so relaxed about my style because I had hand-me-downs as a kid. I was always playing out in the street, wearing these massive dummy t-shirts – they were real big t-shirts, man. But it seemed cool, because I was a kid. Mum did always get me new football boots, though, every time I needed them – both Robert and me got them; she made a point of doing it. Everything else we wore was football tops, big football socks and the stuff my dad sold in the market stalls, like t-shirts and these shirts with these bloody round necks, man – they were called turtleneck tops. They had a high neck, like a turtle's neck, I guess. I remember every single person on the street ended up wearing them because they were selling them in red, blue, green, black, white. That was a funny little thing, but I just thought all that was the norm. I just thought it was normal junk mate, but I do get that some people would think it was mad. To be fair, looking back, I was probably struggling a bit on the style front, but I loved all of my clothes – I didn't care, man.

Then when I was about 17 and started trying to get into clubs – using a fake ID, pretending to be 18 – I always dressed smart: in fitted stuff, looking well-groomed. I was always presentable – ironed shirt, ironed jeans, always smelling nice – but then I'd be in the clubs and just thinking, "Everyone looks the same." Every single person in a fitted white shirt, a pair of skinnies or trousers, a skinny tie and maybe a little cardigan. I just felt, "This is fucking boring, man." It was like walking into a poor man's Ralph Lauren photo shoot.

I was the first one of all my mates to wear ripped jeans, and obviously I got all my mates' dads digging me out: "You fell down, you fell on the floor!" – the same old joke. I was also the first of all my friends to wear skinny jeans. At first, I used to get the piss taken out of me for them; then my mates started saying, "Where did you get them from?" Then they started wearing them. The same happened with the shirts; they would dig me out to begin with, then be like, "Where did you get them from?"

I don't care about fashion brands. No preference as to who makes my t-shirts whatsoever, as long as they're oversized – if it ain't broke and all that. But I do have certain rules for t-shirts and shirts: I'm not keen on buttons on t-shirts, I always roll my sleeves up, that looks cool, and usually go for shirts with mad colours and crazy stuff on them, because I like to stand out. The t-shirt just can't be clingy in any way. It's not a good look. I also always wear skinny jeans, mostly because that's what works best with an oversize tee – it's a nice contrast. I like the jeans that have the rips in them, I think that look is brilliant!

I wear a lot of invisible socks, but only with jeans and trainers. If I am wearing shorts, I always wear long white socks with sandals – it's a very good look. Oh, and the long socks must be Adidas with three lines on. So when I said I don't care about brands, I don't, until it comes to my socks, then I care a lot! My trainers have always got to be clean; I mean perfectly spanking clean. I use a spray called Crack Protect to keep them nice, but I have got a lot of trainers that I don't wear a lot anymore because they're running out of freshness. I also like wearing a snapback – the only ones I wear are

East End Clobber, though, obviously. And watch out for trainers, tracksuits and swimwear coming to an online store near you very soon.

If your clothes are fly, your sexy body should be too, so I use a nice moisturizer on my face and lotion on my body because I like to feel all soft. The other reason I use moisturizers is because I do like a sunbed. The one local to my house is open until 9pm, so I try to pop in there a few times a week in order to keep that healthy glow – I can't be doing with that fake tanning nonsense.

As far as jewellery is concerned, I always wear a long silver chain because that completes the look. I like ones that mean something to me. I've got some little pendants that friends gave me when I was 16, and a fake Tiffany heart – that's one of my favourite. I think it's alright to wear moody things sometimes, especially if they mean something to you.

Then, of course, there are the tattoos. Now, I think tattoos are very cool – I got my first one, Midas, when I was 23 and in Australia. It signifies the "Midas touch" – because everything I touch turns to gold. It was inspired by a school lesson, when we were all sitting on the carpet one day (including Sullivan Shield, who always used to fart on the carpet) and the teacher told us the Greek Myth about the person with the Midas touch, where everything he touched turned to gold. When I heard that I was like, "Wow. I want to be that guy." (Even though I think in the end he turned his wife to gold and was quite pissed off about it.)

My latest tattoo is the Joker because I got my face painted like the Joker when I was in the *Big Brother* house – I also think he's a lot like me. For example, the tattoo has the Joker saying, "why so serious". People compare me to the Joker a lot; I think it's because I can have normal conversations with people, but also I can have really crazy conversations – deep, meaningful ones, which gives me another edge. No one knows how to take me, a bit like the Joker; so he's cool man – the Heath Ledger one. He's the best one – he even died playing that role, he literally went insane making the film; which I think is quite memorable. He took his role so seriously, he died for it.

I've got 22 tattoos in total, and they all mean something to me. I'll take you through a few on a trip round my body: I've got a little diamond on my little finger that basically represents "diamond in the rough". The skull on my hand is one I haven't really seen anyone else with – well I've seen it on one person. When I was looking at tattoos on hands, one come up with a skull and I just thought, "Whoa, that's actually quite cool." The jaw matches the line of my jaw on my face – it took a while to match it up. The skull basically means that I can see through people, I can see if they're good people or bad people. That is the whole point of this tattoo: I think I'm a very good judge of character. The thing is that tattoos on the hand hurts the most, and they don't take as well. They fade a lot quicker than those on the other parts of the body because you're always using them, and it's a different kind of skin, apparently.

I got my crown tattoo because I think I'm the king, I'm the best – yes, a bit sad. And I've got a lion on my other hand because

I feel I'm brave like a lion … "Roar". Then up the arm we've got "love". I want to find love one day, true love. And further up we've got a clock with no hands on; this basically means time doesn't exist, clocks do. Clocks exist, time doesn't. I feel like we're governed by time in this world; telling us when we should get out of bed and whatever, because of a fucking clock. Shut up clock, go away. Live for the moment. Do everything that you want to do now, don't be scared.

I've got a few ladies on my arm … one, two, three, four birds! Yes, man. On my other arm, I've got "Veni Vidi Vici", which means "I came, I saw, I conquered". That's a quote by Julius Caesar, he was a roman emperor.

There's one on my wrist and my left hand that says "Om". It's a Buddhist mantra and it's the vibrations of the universe. Apparently, we're all controlled by the vibrations – the good vibes, they have good feelings, and the bad vibes have bad feelings. I like the temperament of it and I think Buddhists are pretty cool – they're certainly really cool in their dressing: bald fellas in robes, you know what I mean? It looks like my dad.

That's just a few of my tattoos, and I'm always looking at getting more. I have a tattoo TV show coming up, so I'm bound to get a cheeky few more on there surely. But I would never get any on the face, my mum wouldn't like it and she made my face so she sort of has the final say there. I think I just want to work on my left arm now.

I appreciate that the "nail varnish look" is sort of a weird look –
"He wears nail vanish, he must be gay." But I watched *Pirates
Of The Caribbean* and Johnny Depp carries off the nail varnish
when he's filming, so why shouldn't I feel a bit like a pirate,
too? And a bit of Disney princess, as well – it's so bad, I think
it looks cool.

With my hair, I love a nice, slicked-back barnet. I like it long
on the top and short underneath. I always give it a good run-
through with my tangle-teaser comb, then I use VO5 hair putty
and do it all combed back. I loved it when I bleached my hair in
the *CBB* house, especially when I put the blue through it – how
cool was that? I like to mix it up a bit. It's good to keep people
guessing what you might do next … especially when you don't
even know yourself.

With regards to facial hair, I always like to have a bit of stubble
– I've tried it before and I don't want to be all smooth and shiny.
For me, three days worth of stubble is about right for an audition
– that's my ultimate stubble length. I think, not only is it very
manly, it also shows that you care, but you don't care too much
– you care just enough.

No matter what day it is, where I'm going or what I'm wearing,
I always wear my lucky belt. I wear it with every outfit. It's a
sparkly black one from All Saints and I know it works because
I am lucky every day.

BEARZY'S TOP STYLE TIPS

So I suppose you all want to know my advice for how to look good in a TV audition. I've got all the tricks and they haven't failed me so far …

For starters, no hat or sunglasses when you're in there because they need to see your face and remember it. No dirty, scruffy trainers, either. I recommend always wearing big, bright trainers so that the first thing they say to you is, "Wow, your trainers are cool," so that means good strong colours like orange, lime green, electric blue or bright pink. If you're doing this properly, the trainers need to be Nike – and don't forget your invisible socks. Although I love my trainers, I do still like to look smart: I love a white shirt with some nice jeans and a classy cashmere jumper over my shoulders – it's a bit of an Italian look, I suppose. Some days I dress smartly because I need to, other times I just do it because I like to.

I've worn a leather jacket to every single one of my auditions. It's a bit smaller than my actual size so the t-shirt looks even bigger (and I, therefore, look even better). I also like to have very shiny, white teeth. My top ones I think are okay now, but I've decided

I'm going to get a brace for my bottom ones so my teeth end up dead straight. But if you can't afford to get your teeth done, don't worry, I got far enough with what God gave me, so you can too.

Not many people know this trick, but I always use eye drops – they make my eyes look very sparkly and white. If you go out drinking until late at night or early in the morning, the eye drops get rid of the yellow and the red the next morning when you need to go to work and look fresh as a daisy. The drops I use are called Eyedew and I buy them at Boots.

In auditions, it's also important to remember that whoever's judging you will probably have a nose, so don't forget to smell nice. Personally, I like the Gucci fragrance, or Eros by Versace. I also always wear Calvin Klein pants and recommend giving your willy a good wash – you don't want a smelly willy because who knows when you might get lucky?

UNIT 7: CELEBRITY BIG BROTHER

In this chapter, students will explore why Celebrity Big Brother was such a huge deal for Bear, the difference it made to his life, what his parents thought of his antics in the house and all the gossip you want to know about what actually happened inside the house.

The chapter will conclude with Bear's honest, no-holds-barred thoughts on the CBB cast, and his tips on how you yourself can get on Celebrity Big Brother (hint: you need to be a celebrity).

Students will be tested on the following:

What were those "noises" with Chloe Khan?
What role did R Kelly play in Bear's CBB arrival?

BEAR ON CELEBRITY BIG BROTHER

The prospect of *Celebrity Big Brother* in 2016 blew my mind, maybe even more than I blew everyone else's when I got in there. I'd been a fan of the show since it started, so I was absolutely psyched when my agent at the time told me they'd got in touch and wanted to meet with me (join the queue guys).

I knew I'd have more personality than any other *CBB* contestant, not just on this season, but of all time – if you want a big fuck-off show, it's pretty obvious I'm the man to ask. Usually it's the big characters that end up going out first on *CBB*, but I was determined that with me, there'd be no chance that was going to happen. I knew I had it in me to last the duration, and I definitely knew I had it in me to wind people up.

When I went for a meeting with three of the *CBB* execs I was very excitable, and whenever I was talking they were laughing their heads off at me. Of course, I ended up getting a bit carried away, and told them to get some shots in. "Come on, let's make an afternoon of it!" I suggested, but they didn't fancy it. After the chat, they said to me, "Well, we don't usually do this but we're going to give you an offer today, of £12,000. It's the same fee as reality stars that have been in before you got, so it's fair." In all honesty, I wanted to be in that house so badly, I'd have done the whole thing for free. But that was their final offer anyway, so I agreed. Signing all the contracts took ages, and I was away in Portugal with Lillie at the time; feeling nervous and waiting for it all to come through. But even at that first meeting with the execs, although I knew I'd annoy everyone in there, I also just knew that not only would I be in that house, but I'd be in there until the very end. I could tell they believed me that I was the new big star of their show.

It was around then that I decided it was time to change my agent, and left the management I was with to go with someone else, just because I felt like it was the right time. I knew that it would be *CBB* that made me a household name and make me a lot of money, and I wanted to make the most of it. I've earned £500k since coming out of the *CBB* house, and that is only so far. I can hardly believe it – imagine if I'd known this when I went to Thailand with my mates when I couldn't afford a fucking peanut. Now I feel like I've conquered the world, and I've got a lot more steam left in me.

On the day before I left for the house, all my family was at home with me, telling me, "Don't cause too many arguments. Don't be annoying, be funny. Get with someone if you can. Don't make a drama. Keep yourself looking clean and well," I got a variety of different advice. But I knew I'd do what I always do: behave the way I want to and do whatever my gut tells me to do – I know I'm always right.

For my entrance, I wasn't taking anyone's advice. I planned a massive shocker that would get the crowd talking, and leave the people sitting at home gobsmacked. I was blindfolded in the back of a cab sitting with my chaperone, getting totally revved up listening to The *World's Greatest* by R Kelly on a loop. "I think I've made it, I'm the world's greatest!" I was singing to myself, psyching myself right up. The driver was laughing at me, but he's only human. If you listen to that song, it's like it was actually written about me. I still imagine that it is:

I'm that star up in the sky
I'm that mountain peak up high
Hey I made it, hmm
I'm the world's greatest

I'm that little bit of hope
When my back's against the ropes

I can feel it, hmm
I'm the world's greatest

I am a giant
I am an eagle oh
I am a lion
Down in the jungle…

… I am also a BEAR. That isn't in the song, though.

My grand entrance was almost upon me and I was thinking, "I am the fucking greatest, let's put on a fucking great show." I stood in the wings so excited that I felt like shouting before I'd even got on there. I'd decided I would go out wearing sunglasses because it gave off an air of "who is this guy, he's so cool and mysterious". The persona I was trying to give off was someone strolling down the beach looking sexy and like they don't give a fuck, which I'd obviously had loads of practice at. I had a Hawaiian shirt on and I looked the bollocks. It was the kind of shirt I thought would make people think, "This ain't a big deal to him at all," but according to social media, what a lot of people actually thought was, "He's on drugs." Anyway, those big doors were in front of me and I could hear my VT sounding amazing. Then the doors opened, and I had my hand over my face showing my skull tattoo – people may have thought I was off my head on drugs (bit rude), but the truth was that I'd actually drunk about 12 Red Bulls and was on the verge of a heart attack.

So out I strutted, the crowd was going absolutely mental, and Emma Willis was waiting and smiling at me; but also looking a bit nervous. Straight away I thought to myself, "This bird don't like me much, but never mind." So, I ignored her and said to the crowd, "Lob your money on me everyone, 12 to 1. You won't be sorry. Lump it all on me … Where's my dad and my brothers?" Then Emma asked me a question, I took off my sunglass and thought, "This is easy. Next question …"

In the house, I didn't want to come across as fake, and I was never going to talk behind anyone's back because I don't do that anyway, so that meant I was going to be myself whatever happened. On a show like this you need to remember that you want to cause controversy anyway, so if you do have a problem with someone, you get ruthless and say it in front of everyone, you know, put on a show.

People like to ask the same questions all the time when it comes to *CBB*, and there's one question that comes up time and time again: did you have a game plan? The answer to that is, OF COURSE I DID. My game plan was simple: to get as much airtime as possible. And, luckily for everyone watching, I know what makes great TV, end of. I know what gets people talking: don't be bitchy, be fun. But I had already said to myself that I would disagree with people if I genuinely didn't think they were right and say it to their face, all the time. Because, in life, I think it's important if you believe something different to what you hear, you should always say it.

Did I make a bit of a show and do silly things to get on TV? Of course I did, and this is my biggest tip for success: make the show revolve around you. Things like that day in the garden,

I tripped up with the eggs because I wanted to get on telly. I knew everyone would know I did it on purpose, I made that obvious! But guess what? It became "The Bear Show", like I knew it would be – I got through six votes to be the winner, because there was a method to my madness.

I coped with everything that was thrown at me in that house, even when my ex-girlfriend, Lillie, came in. I couldn't believe that. Everyone was getting to see the people they loved on that task, so there I was thinking my dad was coming out – and Lillie came out instead. Fucking gutted. If she had really cared about me that much, she would have had more respect for me than to do that. A girl called Georgia didn't go on *EOTB* because she had more respect for me than to say bad things about me on telly – you can't say that about the stunt Lillie pulled on me, but I guess it didn't do me any harm. Still won the thing, didn't I? My plan when she arrived was to come out, have a coffee and talk about things properly; but the fact that she came on MY show to mug me off – say horrible things about me, talk about all these bullshit promises – well, it just made me know for sure that Lillie wasn't for me.

In the house, people were so desperate to win. They'd sit there and tell me how to win this game. Renee was the worst for doing that, but we all know that she was after me. In all honestly, she did put the moves right on me. She lay in bed next to me and asked me what I thought of Lewis and Marnie, and then said, "We could have a show-mance, you and me." I was just thinking to myself, "What, with you love? You having a laugh?" But I am a gentleman, so I didn't say that out loud. I obviously knew straight away that there was no way in hell that I was up for that, but then she started stroking my chest – which was so awkward – so I just told her that I had a girlfriend, which, as we all know, was true of course – perfect way to get out of that one (thanks Lillie).

But in the end, Renee said some pretty nasty stuff about me. Not much offends me, but when it comes to insulting women about sensitive things I do NOT like it when people say that I've done that because I would never, ever sink that low. I can't believe what she said about me "playing on" her being a victim of domestic violence. What kind of man would do such a thing? As someone who has been bought up with such great morals and respect for their mum, I was very upset by that. Ultimately, I think it was very obvious that Renee needed a bit of man love and was very disappointed that those ever-so-special cuddles were never going to come from me.

One of the highlights of the whole experience for me was in the last few days when my mum, Linda, came in. She's not used to so much excitement and was very nervous. My mum works in a school at lunchtimes, and no one knew that I was her son before that! When the new term started, Mum was shocked at how many little kids watch the show – it's on very late, after all, and naughty things happen – so she went a bit red, I think. Saying that, I've thought about it and there are far worse things on TV at an earlier time. For example, nothing I did was as bad as Max being buried alive on *EastEnders* was it? Still, I know Mum said to the Year 3 kids, "I hope you didn't watch that!" (Especially the Chloe stuff!)

I fancied Chloe from about day nine or ten, once I'd got to know her a little. She'd come from nothing and had a lot of money, as well as being a single mum; and I admired that about her. I thought, "She's a strong girl … and she's got on *Big Brother*." Chloe was very easily led, though – she would jump on the bandwagon when it came to other people's opinions, and I know that's often a sign of weakness and of just wanting to fit in. I always like people to stay true to themselves, even if sometimes that means telling someone something that they don't want to hear.

There's obviously been a lot of speculation as to what happened between Chloe and I in there, mostly because of the baby wipes and the … noises (which made me feel like a bit of a legend). So, to put matters straight: the truth is that we didn't shag. What happened was I fingered her a bit in the toilet, and she sucked me off in the shower (that's what the "baby wipe thing" was about stickiness). It was one of the best blowjobs I've ever had, but not as good as the ladyboy in Thailand – if Chloe had been a man once (I know for a fact that she wasn't), she might've been the winner. The day after she sucked me off I had decided that I was going to 100 per cent bang her – I didn't care if we were on telly or not, it was definitely going to happen. But what happened instead? She went and got bloody evicted! I was gutted. We were going to seal the deal in the shower (splish splash and whoopdee-do) but sadly it wasn't to be.

I must admit, after Chloe left the house I felt a new lease of life – I was like a beast unleashed, because I knew that I'd be so bored, I wouldn't be able to stop myself acting up. Nobody liked me in there but I didn't care. I wanted to make a show for the viewers, and keep winding the rest of the house up. So when I was on my own, without Chloe, I annoyed them even more. When I got out of the house, I had management telling me straight away that it wasn't a good look for me to be with her and that we shouldn't knock about together. I wanted to take her on a few PAs with me but everyone said that I wasn't allowed. It was upsetting, but I just told myself that the people around me knew what they were doing and that they knew best. I didn't know what to believe about Chloe for a while when I got out, because I'd been in a mad house for a month.

But what happened was that every day I was booked up with work, so it turned out that we couldn't see each other and she just went really cold on me. It was a weird feeling; I thought she really wanted to hang out with me. We were supposed to go to a health spa one day, but she was obviously starting to get the hump with me always putting off meeting up with her because she took ages to reply to texts. So I thought "Fuck this, she ain't interested," and I asked Jemma Lucy to come with me instead. After taking Jemma there, we ended up seeing each other, and then Chloe got together with Ashley. I hope it works out for them, but I did like Chloe a lot. Still, if she'd liked me so much, what's she fucking Ash for? I messaged Ashley to try to find out. "Are you banging Chloe?" I asked. He didn't reply. I helped him out with paid tweets recently so that was rude. Everything is so accelerated in the house, so it felt like Chloe and I were together for ages – it'll be interesting to see what happens when we do meet.

The house also gave me a lot of time to think about things to do with relationships generally, including my one with Lillie. I thought she was probably a bit fame-hungry. I thought about little things that had happened between us, and her past exes, and it was in that house that I decided we were done for good.

Even though I was put up for nomination every week by my housemates (from the very first week of the show), I survived the evictions every single week, thanks to the public. I had no idea that I was making headlines almost daily in national newspapers about my "wild antics". On the final night in the house, everyone was excited and nervous. I'd been up for eviction five times and suddenly I thought to myself, "That's pretty good actually ... fuck me, what if I win? There's a nation of people who have been voting for me every week, and are still voting for me now." One by one, I watched the rest of the housemates drop like flies. I mean, I knew I'd beat Renee, Frankie and Aubrey – I was well chuffed about getting rid of those mugs before I'd gone out. But I thought it would be between Marnie and me at the end (I thought every person from *Geordie Shore* won, you see). But it ended up being between Ricky and me. I thought Ricky was so rubbish, and must have been fucking dull to watch, but when we got down to the last two, I decided to just walk out if he was announced the winner. No interview, nothing. I'd have just gone straight home. And then got on a plane to the Bahamas. No press, nothing. Just go away. It would have been an outrage – he didn't deserve to win.

But then I started to think, "Hang on a minute – him versus me? Not a chance mate; I'm going to win this!" And that's when they said my name, and I jumped up. Ricky went to shake my hand but I thought, "I don't care about him," and jumped on Debra the Zebra – my best friend in the house. That moment was so magical, all the lights in the house went from pink to gold. It was a memory I'll have forever; wow, it was so good. And the countdown from ten was like the biggest buzz you've ever had. I don't think I'll ever, ever get a buzz like that again. As I walked down the stairs I saw all my mates, spotted the Geordie Shore lot and all my family. Everyone was screaming my name and I LOVED it. Then, within minutes, I got pulled in for my interview with Emma. Well, WTF was her problem? She didn't like me, and she was furious that I'd won. I couldn't believe how rude she was. She tried to make me look like a bad person rather than congratulate me as the winner. She tried to paint a bad picture of me, and in the end people were saying that she should have been sacked. Maybe she has been sacked now. No dramas anyway, she was going against a whole nation. "Give me a serious interview," she told me. "Bring back Davina McCall," I felt like saying.

When I came out of there after being cooped up all that time it took me a long time to come back to reality – I couldn't wake up from the dream of the house. But when I did, it felt like the world was my oyster (and I had more money in the bank than ever). Everyone told me afterwards they thought I was mad going in with that cocky attitude, but did it work? Course it did, you bellends.

So, here's what I thought of the *CBB* cast:

Lewis and Marnie: Loved them both. My time in the house wouldn't have been the same without those two. I hope they go the distance, I really think they will. They are a beautiful little couple.

Chloe: Loved her, what a real soul she is. I enjoyed my time with her and the naughty things we did. No regrets. We never did get together after the show because we were both too busy but I wish her all the best with her new fella, I really do.

Renee: Hated her, what a jealous bitch. She still talks about me. Fucked up, mate. She spent so much time and energy worrying about what I was saying and doing, that she wasted her time in that house. She might have had a good time if she'd spent less of it watching my every move, ready to strike. I heard she checked into rehab for depression just recently, though, so regardless of the bad words between us, I still genuinely hope that she is okay and that she gets better soon.

Katie Waissel: Didn't like her, she was muggy. Sat on the fence just to be safely in with the cool crowd, or what she thought was the cool crowd anyway. Not an actual pop star, and didn't really have anything to bring to the table.

Aubrey: She was fiery and she hated that I was more funny and likeable than her. I played to her ego, telling her, "You're the best singer ever etc.," – but as a person you're a cunt. She compared me to "herpes" – who even does that? It's a disgusting thing to do. There are people out there with actual herpes who must have been very offended by her being so nasty.

Frankie: False. I kept thinking, "Just be you, mate," but he couldn't be. He was always trying to say the right thing to people, then contradicting himself. He thought he was going to win, I think. No chance.

Sam Fox: What the actual fuck is she about? Who does that bird think she is? I'm sorry, but she got her tits out for a living for years, then goes around judging everyone else. She'd say things to me like, "There you go, you can put that in your book one day, if you ever get one … ha ha ha." Well, here you are, love, I'm showing you, here's the book, and I've put it in it, "ha ha ha". I mean, this is the woman that carries a special pen around with her at all times to sign people's autographs, usually before they even ask her because she thinks she is that special. It's embarrassing, love, and your singing is shit. Go back to the holiday camps, darling, and take your leather jacket with you.

Saira: To be honest, I found her very weird. Strange girl. One of the things she said to me was, "Bear, are you ever violent?" She just decided from the off that because I was an East London boy and a little bit loud, that I was some little thug. I've never been in trouble in my whole life (except with my mum). I thought, "What the fuck you on about, are you the police? I wouldn't call you in a fucking emergency."

Grant: Didn't like him much, he was boring. What did he ever do but cheat on Anthea Turner or something? I don't remember much about her except she likes cleaning. Anyway, to be honest, I was glad Grant fucked off early because he was dull, man.

Biggins: Boring. Once, I jumped on his bed and he said, "Oh fuck off!" He was very showy and two-faced, he believes his own hype and everyone plays to him, but I didn't like him.

Ricky: I hate him. He was jealous as fuck that I was cool. And his acting is shit, too. Yeah sure he was on EastEnders, but they sacked him. Nah, bore off mate. He is so boring, and I was so nice to him, and it was so fucking boring having to be nice to him.

BEARZY'S TOP TIPS FOR GETTING ON CBB

The reason I won CBB is because of my values and my morals. If someone was slagging someone off in one room, I'm not going to join in for the sake of it, that's muggy. In *Big Brother*, if I didn't like someone, I didn't go and talk about them behind their back – I just said it to their face. I'd say, "I don't like you mate, but let's not stew on it. We'll shake hands and move on." That's the way to deal with life. Most of them hated me for that. At one point or another, every single person in there slagged me off. I really couldn't give a monkey's. I knew from an outsider's perspective that what I was doing was true and right for the viewers – I knew they'd see my honesty and morals. They knew I was alright.

UNIT 8: GIRLS

*This chapter is dedicated towards those students who
are wondering why they're not pulling. Bear explains his
straightforward secret to success with the ladies, an overview
of his dating experiences, what he has learned from them
and what you can learn form them too. Based on the
information provided, pupils are encouraged to participate
in some controlled experiments of their own.*

Please note: *Students should expect to be tested on how
the laws of probability can be employed in clubs to ensure
you pull the right girl.*

BEAR ON GIRLS

I've always really loved women, particularly clever ones, like
I said. I love their banter and their lovely hair – especially when
it smells fresh and nice (such a treat). But I do find it confusing
that people always ask what my secret with girls is, because it's
simple: just talk to them. All you've got to do is speak to them,
but you'd be surprised how many blokes actually find that truly
difficult – what do they think's going to happen? The ground isn't
going to open up and suck them down – more likely they're going
to get sucked off; so give it a go, I say.

I was 18 when I got my first girlfriend, Sunigal Senjack. I really,
really liked her, and it was the first time I properly felt like

someone's boyfriend. I honestly felt like I had a bird, and
that made me the man – proper caveman feelings. At the
time I was on £200 a week, and had decided to save up to
get her a nice treat: I'd booked us a weekend at a really posh
health spa. We were about five months into our relationship,
and I was so excited to tell her about it and take her away.
I thought, "This is it – I've found the one, and I'll knock her
socks off with this weekend." Two weeks after that, she dumped
me. RUTHLESS. I was absolutely heartbroken – I thought she
was the love of my life. I will never forget how that made me
feel and I found it really hard to trust girls for a long time after
that. I always had my guard up because I never wanted to feel
like that again.

But ultimately, it didn't stop me from having more girlfriends,
and I've obviously had a fair few relationships over the years –
some meaningful and memorable, some a complete waste of
time. But I do believe that everyone comes into your life for
a reason, even if they play just a little, crappy role in it.

I've honestly never had the money to attract any gold-diggers,
but I've had girls who've cost me a lot of money. One was
Anna, who I met on *Shipwrecked*. I had no money at that point
in time, but you didn't need money for *Shipwrecked* – you're
on an island, you just need to survive. But when we got back
it turned out she was used to going out in London, spending
loads of money. She's quite rich, and she got everything she
wanted. But when the money dried up, she was nowhere to
be seen. And there I was buying fucking drinks for 15 to 20
quid a pop in a London nightclub, really trying. It used to take

a lot – too much, I couldn't afford it. She's a model – she
was Miss London 2010 – and anyone who enters Miss
London or Miss World, it's an ego thing. I'm not being
funny ... has this world gone mad? People actually enter
these competitions?

If you're trying to watch out for girls who want your wallet,
it's good to know that girls who just hang around in clubs
near your table either only want you for a shag – which,
I don't know about you, but I'm not really moaning about –
or they want your money. It's just very hard to tell which
without spending some money. But girls that go out every
single weekend and circle around those tables, they get a
reputation, and they're the sort of girls who want us. A couple
of years ago, they would probably have got a lot of money out
of me, but now I can't really trust anyone. There are always
exceptions, because obviously looks can be deceiving and
I could totally misjudge girls, but girls who don't sleep with
me on the first day, they're the ones to look into. When they
come hungry and you sleep with them, nine times out of ten
it doesn't work out. So make me wait a little bit, but let me
take you home; nothing is going to happen, we'll have a
kiss, no tricky fingers anywhere, just a kiss, I promise.

Then there's the other kind of girl who doesn't necessarily
want your money, but she wants some of your limelight.
For example, Kaley Morris. She loves a picture everywhere
she goes. She just wants to be in the *Daily Mail* but I thought
she was my mate, I thought we got on all right. Turns out,
when I was in *Big Brother* she couldn't wait to slag me off,

just for a silly story. People like that I find embarrassing –
and also, they sleep with everyone. Every single person you
can think of.

With some birds I go on dates with now, I'll be talking to them
and then they go on Snapchat and turn their phone towards me
and then back to them again, waiting for a fruitful conversation.
I'm sitting there thinking, "This is fucking weird." Then they
turn the camera back on to me and it's like, "Are we on a first
date? Yes. So fuck off and put your phone away." For me, that's
rude. I'll do that sort of thing when I'm on the piss to be social
or whatever, but not on a one-on-one date when I'm trying to
get to know someone. It just means they want everyone to
know they're sitting next to me – that's what I'm dealing with
at the minute, and it's so frustrating. Which brings me to my
next point: sometimes I wonder if I have to have a reality star
girlfriend now? Obviously, you can't tar all girls with same
brush; but some of these reality stars only want to be with
you because of who you are as well, which helps their profile.
Then normal girls who haven't been on TV talk about *Ex On
The Beach* and *Big Brother*, and they say to me, "Oh, so how
did you go on to it? Do you reckon I could go on there?" And
I'll be just like, "I'm not going there," and think, "Okay, this
ain't really what I want." All I really want is to get to know you,
whether or not you're a fan. I don't really want you to go on
Ex On The Beach, because I would like to see you. It's just
a bit crazy in that sense.

But there is a girl called Briney, Briney Dockerty. She's cool.
Basically, I've known her since I was 18, and it's been on and

off since then. She's nice, she's genuine, she lives down the road and she knew me before all this TV lot. But she never gives me big edge. She never talks about it, and we'll just talk about normal things – which I think is quite big, because it is pretty obvious and you may want to talk about TV stuff. But it's good to just talk normal to me, about normal things. I like girls like that; who don't really care about Snapchat or social media or getting pictures with me and telling her friends she's meeting up with me – those who want a bit of the fame or to say they've slept with me, or whatever it is.

That's why I've gone to my next plan: the only birds I can see are ones with a real genuine career; like a singer or actress or someone like that. I would love to fall in love with a singer. I don't know what it is; maybe it's their confidence and the way that they are. They've got true talent, because singers work really hard and I like girls to keep me on my toes. Obviously I want them to text me back straight away, and I want to text back to what nice girls say, but in all honesty, I find nice girls kind of boring – in the sense that I don't like quiet girls. When I introduce them to my family, they've got to have a bit of a voice, something about them, an edge. Not girls that just say "yes" to going everywhere. Like if I would suggest "Oh babe, do you want to go play mini golf?" I want a girl that's going to reply, "I don't really like mini golf, let's go bowling." I'd like someone with a bit of a backbone. I need girls with something about them.

The last girl I was truly in love with was Vicky P. I worshipped the ground she walked on, and we had such a laugh. I remember a few months into our relationship we went to Ibiza together.

Vicky
Before

Wehey
Pet!

One night on the island we had this evening of wild, wild sex; the next day we were supposed to go to this club called Zoo, but we'd had such a smoochy night that the next day her hair was all clumped up in knots. The knots were so bad – like proper dreadlocks – that they couldn't be combed out, so in the end I had to sit on the bed and cut her hair with a knife to get them out. It looked so terrible that we ended up not going out!

The moral of this story is: don't let me cut your hair. Especially when I'm using a kitchen knife and my head is in Ibiza mode.

One of the things about Vicky was that she would always be on her phone, and sort of ignore what people were saying. That annoyed me a little bit, because when I go into someone's house I put my phone in silent and I won't even look at it. But she would start going on her phone in front of my family while they were talking. I just thought, "That's a bit rude." One time, she went on her phone and I went mental – I was already mad with a lot of the things she did. Then my brother and Vicky went out, and Danny went, "Is she on coke?" I was like, "No, she is not. It's just her." It was so funny, none of my family liked Vicky. They said I could do better than her. And, actually, I could do better than her. She would never stick up for me. She would post pictures of boys on their social media, and tag them and say, "Lovely day with so and so." I would never do the same thing. If I'm seeing someone, I don't want to give any other girl a look-in. But that was just her, and my family felt that she was sort of mugging me off. Then she would say things on her phone to me like, "You are only with me because of who I am." And I just thought,

"Who the hell are you to say that to me?" You are no-one.

She changed her tune when I won *CBB*, though. She even
pretended that she hadn't watched it when blatantly she had –
made me laugh that. She's just bitter because she's missing the
Bearzy-love; she knows that she's missed out on the greatest
life ever with me, but that's her problem now. She missed her
chance. If I wanted to, I could get back with her, but I don't want
to and that kills her. I'd be like, "Alright babe?" if I saw her, but
she'd be shouting and going mad.

The main problem with Vicky in our relationship was that she
was very, very controlling. She still tries to control me now; like
she says I talk about her "all the time", then leaves me voice
messages calling me a "fucking freak", which isn't very nice.
And if she finds out someone is my friend, or that they follow me
on Twitter, she instantly falls out with them. All she's doing is just
making it obvious that she's still in love with me. I know that she
is, but I also know that she'd never admit it. Anyway, Vicky's not
my cup of tea anymore – she posts photos of herself online with
all these other boys because she thinks it makes me jealous.
It's all quite immature, really. Then she slags me off in the press
and calls me "the most vile and manipulative person she's ever
met." I was so nice to that girl, and it makes me feel so sad.
I think she's worth more than that and I still care for her, and I
do want to ring her up and just go, "Babe just calm down a little
bit. You've got so much more to offer, just don't lose your head
and everything will be okay." I still do care about her, but I know
for a fact that if I were to ring her up she would start telling
everyone, "Bear rang me ..." and just rub it in my face.

I would like to see her, actually, because obviously she's got such a big opportunity at the minute, but I'm scared that she's going to blow it. And the people that are surrounding her, they're not even her friends – even when I used to see her, I told her straight, I said, "Those people you're knocking about with, babe, they're not your mates; they don't actually care about you." And that's why I think she's going through a rough time at the minute. But, like I said, it's not my place to say anything, which is a bit of a shame because the truth is, Vicky actually came to live with my family and I for an entire month because things weren't going too good for her at home. My mum and dad treated her like their daughter, she wanted for nothing, and I went around cleaning her fucking knickers from the bathroom when she left them in there – these are the things that she doesn't mention to the press. God forbid that people might think that I'm actually quite nice. Really she should be thanking me after my family and I looked after her, but there you go – I'm a gentleman and I'm not going to say anything bad about her, ever. The feelings will always, always, always be there with Vicky and me.

Like I said before, I know she does love me still, but it's a shame that I can't just put it on the straight and narrow like I want to, because I think Vicky is massively letting herself down at the minute. Everyone's talking about it. I've seen some clips of interviews and it's just not her. Two years ago, Vicky would never go to do an interview hanging from the night before, still a bit drunk or whatever. I don't think she's being very professionally at the minute – not because she thinks she's "made it", just I don't think she's as professional as she once was. I don't think she's hungry for it anymore and she thinks she can just turn up, joke about and leave. I generally believe that Vicky thinks she's done enough, but at the end of the day you've got to still look professional because it's such a small industry, and everyone talks. Vicky could do so well. She is a very nice girl; that's the shame of it all really. Obviously, we broke up for a reason, but she's got some really good qualities … then again, she's also got some really bad qualities. And I think she needs to have a re-think about the people she surrounds herself with.

As everyone knows, I was seeing Lillie when I went in the *Celebrity Big Brother* house. Lillie is originally from Birmingham and she goes on lots of nice holidays and stuff; she always looks beautiful and she's got gorgeous hair … and I loved her legs. I obviously like girls who look after themselves, but I can't stand girls when they apply all that make-up like Lillie. She took so long getting ready, and when I wanted to go and kiss her, she'd be like "get off my lips". I think, "Oh, I just want to sling a jumper on and go to shop with a cap on, without worrying what you look like all the time. It's so frustrating."

The thing with Lillie was that, although she definitely did get my banter, it always felt like a little spark, something that I couldn't put my finger on, was missing. I'll openly admit it was a mistake on my part not ending that relationship sooner. I know that I really should have split up with her properly before I went into the house. I did try to – I'd split up with her for a whole day around a month before I went in the house, but I was weak for some reason and I didn't stick to it. I should've, because I knew it wasn't right for me to be in that relationship. Instead, I ignored her calls for 24 hours and then, eventually, rang her back. Like I say, I just need womanly-ness near to me at all times, and I had started to think, "I've just been to Portugal with her, she does actually care about me and has my best interests at heart." So I gave it a bit longer, even though I knew it was wrong, and decided that I'd sort it out when I came out of the house. Me being me, I figured I'd just live for the moment. And that's what I did.

Lillie was a nice girl, until she went onto *Big Brother*. She is fascinated by the media and what everyone is saying about her, and I remember her mum would come and talk about other celebrities with her while I was in bed. I'd be sitting in bed at her place in Birmingham, really late, just talking; then her mum would come in and have a gossip about other celebrities: "Oh, do you know so and so is pregnant?"; "Have you seen a picture of that one in her dress?" And I'm just sitting there thinking, "You lot are fucking sad." You have nothing better to talk about than that? My mum draws a blank on that sort of thing and goes to work. But when those two started talking about celebrities when we were sitting in bed, that was another reason I thought, "This isn't for me, man, it's fucking weird."

So, at the moment I'm single, but I'm always up for the prospect of meeting the new Mummy Bear. You never know who's around the corner, do you? I appreciate it would probably be a little tricky being my wife, but I would never, ever cheat on my wife. I would give her my phone and say, "Look, just have it," because I'd have nothing to hide. I'd give her the passwords to all my emails and social media because I know I'd never be bad to the woman I married. I want to find the girl of my dreams at around the age of 30, which would be a perfect time to start settling down – though, who knows when the right girl will come along? I just know she's out there. I do want kids now, though, because I'm broody. But you've got to watch it, because girls are crafty; probably worse than boys. For example, my mate's girl was with another man for 25 years. Ten years into their relationship, she'd go to America for two weeks at a time, supposedly to ride horses. But guess what? She wasn't riding wild horses, she was riding wild willies – she kept a secret for 15 years. That shit is crafty, man.

In a relationship, I think that if sex stops, you know that things are very wrong. It's literally THE most important thing. That would be game over for me – if it's not happening, it's time to break up. It's going against animal instinct. That's why, if I am being honest, I do like to treat myself to a good prostitute. I don't see a problem with it. I think to myself, if the money is there – why not? The way I look at it is this: if you are going to a nightclub to buy birds drinks, you are effectively doing that to have sex with them anyway, so really, what's the difference? So let's cut out the middleman, and go straight to the prostitute. No fucking about, no Uber in the morning, everyone saves time: there's no Whatsapping, no need for a conversation neither of you really want to have – I think it's fucking great. Some people think it's wrong, but you know what? Some people have one sugar in their tea, some people have two. Personally, I like coffee. What I'm saying is, everyone is different.

The thing about me is, wherever I am in my life, whatever I'm doing, I'm only comfortable if I've got a strong female vibe around me. I've always got to have a girl around me, always. Like in *CBB*, I obviously liked Chloe Khan; it was important for me to have a girl around me. I think I just need lady cuddles – but also because women make me feel relaxed and content and, like I said, girlfriends have inspired me to do well. Vicky was so clever, and Lillie had her own clothing line – but, like Vicky, she's dead-set on just being famous. Regardless of their personal ambitions, however, I'm good at picking girlfriends – I make good choices (they're always clever, so I can learn from them); but when it ends, obviously it's always my fault. When I see them out and about, I'll always say hello, because I'll always have a bit of love for all of my ex-girlfriends, no matter what.

When I do find "the one", I want ten kids and a big house ... and lots of cats. I also want a peacock and a turtle, but don't we all? Ultimately, I know I want to have lots of babies and to be with the same person forever; because you go on a journey together watching your kids grow up, and I think that's beautiful. I also want to make sure I'm completely financially stable when I have children. My parents have been married for 37 years and they are my relationship role models, because they are still so much in love – my dad is even madder than me, so they must be doing something right.

Before I went onto *Big Brother*, let's suppose I fancy this singer, well they wouldn't even look at me before. But now I genuinely believe if I were to approach a singer, and say a good icebreaker, they'd go, "Sugar, you're probably quite funny." I can't word this without sounding really arrogant and really vain, but since I've been in the limelight, I think I'm worthy now. Even if I was worthy before, with my status now, I genuinely believe I could pull any girl. It's so embarrassing to say, but it is what it is, so there you go – this limelight shit has just put me in a whole new level of lady-bracket.

BEARZY'S TOP TIPS FOR PULLING GIRLS

Like I say, the first and main thing about pulling a girl
is to TALK to them – it's not going to happen by magic,
unless you're Harry Potter. With some of my ex birds,
they've obviously just walked out of the sea on a TV
programme and, granted, the way I pulled them was
a bit like magic; but if you're not that lucky, here's a few
ideas to set you off on your way:

Let's imagine you're in a club: hopefully you've already
brushed your teeth, had a shower, got clean clothes
and trainers on, and you are looking fresh to death.
Now you need to set yourself a target and play the
numbers game – the more birds you chat to, the
greater your chances of going home with one of them
… probability is what they call it, don't they? If you do
a nice little circuit of the club and carefully spot the
girls you fancy, talking to each one, you are setting off
a chain of events; and the more girls you approach,
the higher your chances are of one of those events
happening near your willy. Some people say, "Go for the
best birds in the club," others say, "Stick to ones who
you have a reasonable chance with." I say, "You could
increase your chances by actually playing below par," –
but this isn't an approach I've ever favoured myself.

Girls way prefer it when you spend pretty much the whole time talking about yourself and how great you are, so don't bother asking her too many questions. Also, a compliment never goes amiss, especially when it's about her boobs or bum – makes them feel really valued and respected, trust me. By the end of the night you're hoping to take her back to your mum's house for a night of hot love-making, but first of all, you need to make sure you're in with a good chance of getting lucky; so be upfront. Don't mince your words, just explain to her what you'd like to happen between the two of you. It's good for the both of you to be open about where you stand – you don't want to walk her all the way home to have her slam the door in your face, that's a waste of your effort (especially if it's your door!). So you're best off making your intentions clear. Tell her she's going to have the best night of her life, then just do your best to not make it the worst. Alternatively, if you don't want to dive straight in with "I wanna bang you", you can break the ice with the offer of a magic trick. Tell her that one of the many things you learned from watching Paul Daniels as a kid is the disappearing trick. This means that you're amazing at having sex and then disappearing, never to be seen or heard from ever again – she's sure to want a piece of that, ladies go nuts for that shit. It's like catnip.

Last of all, let's talk about alcohol: be honest, we all love it. Be it ten pints of lager, a couple of bottles of cheap plonk or 15 vodka Redbulls followed by tequila shots and several Jägerbombs, we just love to get plastered. But if you actually want to do it correctly, you should have just the right amount to make you seem funnier than you actually are – more confident and more relaxed –but still make sure you're sober enough to reign it in a bit. Don't go too far, as it can oh-so-easily go horribly wrong (trust me). So, know your limits, and watch out for those beer goggles to avoid any nasty shocks the next morning. It's happened to me more than once – I've woken up with some real surprises the next morning, and I'm not talking about the ladyboys again, by the way.

Oh, and last but definitely not least: make sure you wrap up your old fella, because you don't want to end up down the sex clinic a week later with an itch you can't scratch.

UNIT 9: PLANNING FOR THE FUTURE

This chapter contains guidance on questions ranging from: "What am I doing with my life?" to "How do I find the time to start my business?"

Bear will instruct you on how to sort your life out – or at least start planning how to sort your life out – giving his personal experiences of planning for the future, what he hopes for himself, and why he sees a lot of Segways and rabbit hutches in his future.

Includes: *Top tips on how to make your future a little better than your past! (Students are advised not to expect immediate results.)*

BEAR ON PLANNING FOR THE FUTURE

At the moment I'm busy making a documentary about my life. I started filming after I came out of *CBB*, and it's like a "what happened next" type of documentary. I think it'll end up being a real insight into my life: the personal appearances, my life at home, my cats – I've got some interesting characters in there, but you'll have to wait for it to come out to see what I bring to life.

These days, you can make amazing films for hardly any money. In fact, some of the best films have been made on a tiny budget. For example, the film Paranormal Activity was designed to look as if a couple were setting up cameras in different rooms to film evil spirits as they appeared. The cameras were basically used like security cameras, so to the viewer it looked like everything you were seeing was "discovered footage" – pretty clever. Not many people know that was made on a super-low budget – only about $15,000, or around £10,000 – and was an independent film, like mine is going to be. That film ended up earning $193 million for Paramount Pictures; they've made six of those Paranormal Activity films now … incredible. I honestly think that if I put my mind to film-making, I could potentially make millions – I've got real business nous. For example, in my documentary all the venues I use are free: churches, pubs and my house (classic stuff).

With regards to film, I would also like to act – nothing ropey like *EastEnders*; more highbrow stuff, like *Scarface* or *The Godfather*. I would play a gangster and obviously be brilliant at it. I'd wear a suit like one of the Rat Pack; and probably belt out My Way like my dad does when he's pissed …

As far as radio is concerned, personally I think I'm fucking great; but not many people ask me to go on. Maybe they think I'm a liability; they shouldn't, though, because I would never swear on live radio – that would be so rude. Still, I suppose you could say that I'm often a little impulsive, like a few months ago I was sitting with my brother, Robert, in a Costa coffee shop near our house, and randomly I just said, "Cats." Basically, I'd had an

hour's sleep and had started to google "cats in East London".
I looked up and said to Rob, totally seriously, "Let's get some
kittens, today." He looked at me a bit funny (he does that a lot)
and then said, "You can't just get cats." Well, I didn't agree with
this statement (plus, we already had the van outside so we were
basically destined to go and get some cats anyway) so I said,
"Come on, let's get the cats. What else are you doing today?"
And that was it: off we went and ended up at this Asian lady's
house in Ilford.

When she let us in it all felt a little bit shady, to be honest. It
was a scummy place, like a prostitute's house but not as sexy
(plenty of pussy, though). She took us to see the kittens, which
were all in a big pile, and then one jumped out at me – that
was Bearzy – but there was another one that I kept looking
at; he was so fluffy, and I looked into his little eyes and knew I
couldn't leave him. This little guy was Simba, of course; I knew
he was the one for me. I had quite a bit of dosh by then, so I
went to the cashpoint and got out £400 – she wanted an extra
£50 because Simba was SO fluffy, but in the end she let me
take him with his brother. And fucking hell, all of a sudden
we'd got some cats – yes!

My mum and dad went mental at first, but now they love them.
Mum was just angry because I didn't have any food or a litter
tray with me when I bought Simba and Bearzy home; but she
understood that they needed to be rescued when she clapped
eyes on them – honestly, they were at death's door: underfed
and dehydrated. I realise now that they'd come from a kitten
farm, but since they've been with me they are the happiest

little cats. They're the talk of the house – they've even been in the press, they're famous!

I think the cats helped a lot, because we lost our dog Charlie last year. He was ten years old – and I had to bury him! I cried for a week because I was so broken hearted. We all were. I think it knocked me particularly hard, because I remember after I dug him a grave in our back garden; I was sitting next to him just staring at the ground for hours. He'd had a heart attack at the park and it made me think, "What is life?"

Basically, these cats represent how I live: wake up and do what I want – that day, I wanted cats. Maybe tomorrow will be dogs or fish. I like to surprise myself; I don't know what I'm going to do next.

Ideally, I would like to run and own a Segway park, which would also include animals. You could go round on your Segway and see things like peacocks, llamas, giant tortoises and leopards all roaming together in the wild – it would be part of the Bears Tours group that I am setting up. I may put a campsite on the grounds, as well. I think wooden pods might work better than caravans, and then every pod could have its own rabbit hutch. I could get on board with that. I think a lot of people could get on board with that. Who doesn't like bunnies? Even robots like bunnies, and I want to be prepared for the robot apocalypse.

But that idea's going to require some serious planning (and a lot of rabbits), so in the immediate future I'd love to design my own range of teddy bears. I think it's only fair that everyone has the chance to have their very own "Stephen Bear bear" in their life – plus, these one's won't come with such big gobs.

Inspiration is all it takes, sheer genius imagination. If you don't act on the things that inspire you in life – whatever that inspiration is, be it to go travelling, do a painting or open a Segway animal park – you won't get anywhere. People get an idea and it's brilliant but they forget about it, because ultimately they're too scared to put it into action and take the first step; but you've got to be courageous to get anywhere.

Technology has always been one of my greatest loves. I spend most of my life on my phone so occasionally get some time to play some games in between Instagram and Snapchat posts.

It was during one of these moments that I came across Dig That Gold. It's a game where you collect gold, while walking around in a mine. Why this is so good, though, is that the gold you earn in the game adds up to become gold in real life. You heard me right, these guys are giving out free gold for playing a game on your phone!

As the clever, entrepreneurial type, I got in touch with these guys to find out what the crack was and they gave me my own mine in the game. That means if you play the game, you can get rewarded with real gold bars for playing on your phone while sitting on the loo.

Download Dig That Gold in the app store to get started...

UNIT 10: PERSONAL APPEARANCES

This chapter will enlighten students on the behind-the-scenes of what goes into making a personal appearance. Bear will teach you what to ask for, what to expect, exactly how many Jägerbombs to drink, how to deal with hecklers and why you shouldn't get into bed with a load of random strangers on stage*.

This chapter also includes Bear's tips on stage-diving, which students are advised not to practice at home.

*After extensive research, Bear has concluded that loads of random strangers "off stage" is fine.

BEAR ON PERSONAL APPEARANCES

I do a lot of personal appearances in nightclubs and other places – I've done at least one every single weekend since I came out of the CBB house. Personal appearances are known at "PAs" in the 'biz, and this is how it works, for me anyway:

I've got something called a "bookings agent", and it's via this agent that clubs and wherever else can book you for a PA. Then the club and your agent can sort out all the flyers and posters saying what night you're going to be there, how it's a big star appearance, a life-changing experience, etc., etc. All you have to do is keep that day free in your diary and make sure you've got a hotel booked if the PA's going to be far from where you live – basically, just make sure what's happening is whatever works for you.

When the night of the PA comes, I get the car with Clint, my road manager, and we rock up to the club at about 1am. That might sound a bit late to turn up anywhere except bed, but that's the time when clubs are packed. It's also at this time that everyone is at their most drunk, and always love seeing someone off the telly and going, "Waaaaah, look there he is, off the telly." While they're doing that, I go to the VIP area (also known as the "Playas Lounge") and have a drink for half an hour with staff. When I'm out, I always have vodka Redbull and plenty of Jägerbombs, that way I'm at my most "Bear" for everyone who comes and has a picture with me.

It's usually a pretty standard routine with PAs; but one time, I turned up at this club and there was a huge fluffy double bed on stage. I thought it was just a normal PA, but instead, they wanted me to get into the bed and have photos with everyone on the mattress, with the covers over us. I looked at it for a minute and thought, "Hang about … this could be trouble." So I just said, "No way," to the fella. I mean, can you imagine all the stories that would come out about me: "Bear touched me in the bed"? No way. I ain't a mug. But that was an important lesson: to remember you've got to be on the ball in this game, even after several Jägerbombs.

The worst thing about Pas – worse than the bad surprises – are the very few nasty people that want to mug me off. What these comedians do is: waste their night queuing up for ages, then think they're incredibly clever for saying, "I don't even know who you are," to me. But then, you can one hundred per cent guarantee that they'll say, "I'll have a picture with you, though." Mentalists. What they do that for? I think it's rude, just plain unnecessary, in fact. Also, they're spending money to have a night out; do they like to insult people as a past-time and spend money on going out to do it like a sport? That shit is sick if you ask me.

But anyway, it's best not to dwell on the dickheads. The best PA I've ever done was at the Steinbeck and Shaw club in Canterbury, Kent, because I achieved a lifelong ambition there. Something that I had always wanted to do growing up was a proper, full-on stage-dive – and with me, if I want to do something, I'm going to do it; it's just a matter of time. So once I'd got the idea in my head that I was going to do it, no one was going to be able to talk me out of it (they never do). I got my phone out, did a big build-up, prepared everyone on the ground and then took the dive. I went up into the air like a graceful dolphin – and then fell straight to the floor. I couldn't believe it; when I dived, they dropped me. It wasn't exactly the stage-dive that I had dreamed of for all those years, like a stadium-tour-at-Wembley-style one; more a school-tournament-style one. I didn't care, though. I just got up and dusted myself off. I'd wanted to do that since I was 14 and it was the perfect opportunity, but I just wasn't very aerodynamic that night.

Other than falling flat on my face, the best thing about the PAs so far, for me, has been the girls. Oh my God, I have met some really, really fit ones since I've been doing this. And I've also had my first ever threesomes (I've had two of them, and all four of the girls were so hot). One of the threesomes happened when I was doing a PA and got chatting to a couple of really fit birds; one girl was Irish, one was English. We ended up going back to the hotel together, had a little cuddle and then we did the business – and it was spectacular. We got into bed to go to sleep and I thought, "Cor, this is great." I remember I had my arms around them both, and then I think I fell asleep snoring. There and then, I honestly felt like I had completed life, a bit like Henry VIII probably did every night he had a threesome. So, exhausted, I closed my eyes, had a little snore and when I woke up again, I looked around for them in the bed, but they had disappeared. Immediately, I thought, "Where's my phone and wallet?" But everything was there in the room, just as I had left it. They hadn't touched a thing, so they must have just genuinely wanted me for my body that night – what an absolute touch. I couldn't believe that they hadn't fleeced me, and we had had such a good time. So that was quite cool.

Another night when I was doing a PA, I met this one girl and she was beyond gorgeous. When she came and said hello, as she was shaking my hand, she put a condom in it with her number written on it. I thought that was pretty slick – I couldn't think of a move that smooth. In fact, I was a bit taken aback by how slick it was, so I said, "Cheers babe, have a drink here if you want." Obviously, she did want to, and she also wanted to come back to the hotel with me that night. She was so clever, as well as gorgeous; she could speak Swedish, German and English – wow.

Lots of girls catch my eye all the time, but what can I say? Women are beautiful. They smell nice, and being around women makes me happy and relaxed. I fancy the girl who lives next door to me at my mum and dad's house. She works in a food shop near me (it'd be handy if I married her because I'd save on Uber fares). When I'm at a PA, I get four or five offers a night (not for marriage, the other stuff) – I've had more than that some nights, and I've also had just one. I don't take them all up, though, even though it is sometimes hard to choose, if I'm honest. But I never go into a club thinking "Who am I going to have sex with tonight?" That is just disgusting. How I respond to their advances varies depending on how up front they are with me, and girls are just as bad as boys, in my opinion. But I love sex, so I don't mind being used for my body – I like having cuddles, so what's the problem? With the PAs, I've got a hotel paid for, and I'm living the life of Riley. What 26-year-old wouldn't take full advantage of that?

And who is Riley anyway?

BEARZY'S TOP TIPS ON PERSONAL APPEARANCES

I must have done well over a thousand PAs by now, probably more. You could say, on that basis, that I am an expert on the subject and you're learning from the best here ...

If you are in any way faint-hearted, PAs are probably not going to be your thing. I say this because doing these appearances, you have to be prepared to walk into a club and get screamed at, mainly by girls, though, so that's a bonus. If you don't fancy the idea of that, then PAs are definitely not for you. Also, you have to remember that, for all the girls, you do still get the dickheads who literally come along purely to shout abuse at you. And (unfortunately) you can't really just walk up to them and knock them out, so you've got to ignore it and let it go – not always easy.

Doing PAs can also get very tiring; mostly because you have to be prepared to spend a LOT of your time travelling. I can go from one night in Glasgow, to Birmingham the next, to Dublin the next, to Southampton the next – that's a lot of time on the road and in airports, so if you get car sick or plane sick, you might want to swerve PAs entirely. I find all the travelling gives you time to think and come up with new ideas – and, of course, time to sleep, so there are up-sides to it too (including the money).

If you don't mind travelling, you should always make sure that you have a "plus one" at hand – because, who knows? And if you mostly drive to your venues, you need to get yourself a road manager. A road manager is someone who organises how to get you from place to place; they speak with the booking agent to make sure you've got a hotel, and an arrival time, all of that sort of thing, so sort of like a "road mum". Clinton is my road manager/mum and we have a lot of funny times together because we spend so much time with each other. He comes to all my Pas, so it's lucky we get on.

Some famous people like to get a photographer to wait for them outside their hotel, and they tell them when they are coming out so they can look all surprised, like, "Ooh you're taking my photo! I had no idea!", even though they're the one who rang the geezer with the camera and set the whole thing up in the first place. This sort of thing has never really been my style, but I've been out with a few girls who absolutely love it and live for that shit. I think it's muggy, to be honest.

Obviously, I enjoy myself at the clubs – they wouldn't
book me if they thought I was going to get there and
be a miserable, boring arsehole. And that's the main
thing when you are doing a PA: even if you've had a
shit day, and your cat died, you lost a game of Mario
Kart or something really bad has happened, you've got
to stay fun and upbeat, no matter what – that's your job
while you're there. There's obviously a line between not
having enough of a good time and having too much of
a good time, which I struggle with sometimes. But life
is all about balance, and sometimes you have to go to
both ends of the scale in order to restore that balance
(what did I say at the start of this? I'm a fucking guru).
I like to go to different places and be remembered
in that town, wherever it may be, for years to come.
I want to be in people's memories, like:

"Do you remember the day that THE Stephen Bear
came to our town?"

"Err, yeah. It was the most amazing day of our lives!"

I think ultimately, for me, one of the best things about
doing a PA is probably when you get there and there
are genuine fans who have travelled to come and see
you – that is just the loveliest thing. I always try and
give them as much time as I possibly can and invite

them to have a drink with me. People can be so kind, and it warms my heart. The other day, a fella told me that I was the most real, genuine bloke he'd even seen on TV, and that I'd given him confidence to just be himself and always tell people what he thinks of them. This made me so proud; it means there is one less two-faced person in the world, thanks to me.

UNIT 11: AMBITIONS

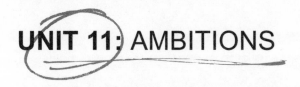

This chapter tackles how to hone your ambitions, why you should have ambitions and what you need to do to make those ambitions a reality. Using Buddhist aphorisms, Bear teaches pupils how hungry for success you need to be to really succeed.

This chapter also details how motivational speeches can help you on the road to success, why it's ok to have a flash car if you've worked hard for it, and the surprising nature of Bear's biggest ambition.

Students will be tested on the following questions at the end of the chapter:

What is the name of the doctor who changed Bear's life?

Is he a real doctor? Or one of those ones like Dr Dre? (Students will have to do their own research for this question, answers not included in textbook.)

BEAR ON AMBITIONS

I feel like my life is only just beginning. I'm so lucky having won *Celebrity Big Brother* – I've been given the means to make opportunities happen for me in my life, and have the freedom to create a vision for my future. From the outside, it may seem like I have a lot of plans, but I have a lot of life to live. I honestly feel like I am just starting on my road to success, and the streets (either side of that road) are paved with gold.

For starters, I've already started my clothing line called East End Clobber. Like I said, I've started off doing caps, but I'm going into all sorts soon. I want it to be the next big clothing chain in the UK – my merchandise is looking so good people can't help but love it.

I'm never short of ideas. I'm constantly getting new ones – there's so much inspiration from my travels. I've never been in a position to execute my ideas before because I've had no money, but now, I'm in a position to do bits and bobs of what I want as I'm earning more. Next thing I'll be doing is my documentary, as I've mentioned before. At the moment, I'm taking the camera with me wherever I go: one day I'll be taking it to Belfast to film a chat show, the next night I might be sitting having a pizza with my niece and nephew … it's diverse. It's surreal, but it's going to be unreal. I can't wait until it gets snapped up for TV, because it will be the biggest insight into who I am that anyone has ever seen.

There are also things I've experienced in life that I have ambitions to retrace. For example, I still want to own a bar in Ibiza, because for me, Ibiza will always be the best place on earth. I want to make the bar there this really special place where the vibe is like nowhere else on the island, and everyone feels the most happy and joyful they've ever felt in their lives – Ibiza helps make you feel like that anyway. There are a lot more ideas I had when I lived there years ago that I'd like to continue; like my boat parties – get that boat rocking again!

I've got some big ambitions for my back garden: I would like to build Disneyland in my back garden. I want fun rides, I want an outdoor gym (what decent theme park doesn't have an outdoor gym?), I want big fancy car shows and I want clowns making balloons. Also, when I get bored, I want to get in my helicopter – no-one else at my Disneyland is allowed in it, though, I'm not a fucking charity – and go for a little spin, and end up at my swimming pool, heated preferably because it's cold. I also want a tennis court, I want a basketball court, I want a hockey field – all in one garden, so you'll never get bored. And don't forget the water slides! We'll have an arcade, and I want a chill-out room like a cinema room, with fluffy blankets everywhere, big fluffy pillows, a projector screen. I also want to employ someone who just gives me massages – they'd sleep at my house, so they best be nice.

I'd like to see the Seven Wonders of the World, wherever they are. I'd also like to do a skydive. You know what, actually, no. I don't want to skydive. I don't want to risk me dying. I don't want to do a skydive, I don't want to bungee jump, but I do want to see the Seven Wonders of the World. And I want to have every single super car: a Ferrari, a Porsche, a Lamborghini, a Bugatti. I want the car Batman's got. I'll get it specially made in black – maybe I'll go see the Seven Wonders in each of my super cars.

My biggest ambition in life is to have a nice big house with a lovely girl and get married. I believe that you find the one, and that's it – done and dusted, you stay together forever. I've got a tattoo with a man and a woman together, wrapped around each other, which means we've got each other's back. And that's what I want the most from a future wife: someone who is there for me not matter what, because you have your hard times as well as your good times, but you've got to know that that person will always be there for you regardless (... and obviously she'll also be gorgeous).

As far as this big house is concerned, I'd like it so big that I could build a helipad; because I would like a helicopter for the roof so I can pop over to Ibiza when I need to, or just go on general adventures. Preferably, I'd like to live somewhere hot, where you can commute to Spain in two-and-a-half hours; so I'd also like to learn Spanish (on audiotape) and have little babies who can all speak Spanish, too –- I'm going to have ten children (just FYI future Mummy Bear).

What I'm definitely going to do is open a shelter for abandoned pets: dogs, cats, guinea pigs, tortoises, goldfish – the lot. The shelter will be all pink and happy, there will be furry cages and I'll call the shelter "Care Bear". I will open a separate one for baboons, because I love them, but they are zoo animals not pets. That would be ridiculous.

Because I'm so ambitious and have such a can-do attitude, people ask me, "Do you ever feel low?" But the truth is, I never get down. My lowest point in life was probably when I broke up with Vicky and she said nasty things about me. I remember one night, I'd been out with Vicky at a PA, and Casey Bachelor went up to her and said, "What are you doing with him, he's got no money?" I can't believe there are girls out there that think like that. Ruthless. I used to walk round the park and listen to motivational speeches to pick myself back up again. I'd tell myself, "Come on mate, there are always worse things going on in this world," which there really are, and I'd get my head back in the game again. I've never been down since, and my plans for the future are to stay happy and excited by life forever.

The speeches that get me in the zone are by a man called Dr Eric Thomas. Now Dr Eric is a very wise man. He's a motivational speaker, an author and a minister, who does talks on the secrets to success. So professional sports teams from the NBA, NFL and MLB in America get him in to their training grounds in order to help inspire their athletes – and they lap that stuff up. He gives them a good talking to so that they perform at the highest level, and he's also spoken to several colleges, schools and companies for the same reason: to inspire, and basically put a rocket up your arse. Dr Eric's had a pretty hard life, but it's because of all the obstacles he's had to overcome that he gives such great advice. I read up on him a bit, and he studied for two years to get this special degree that everyone said he'd never be able to get, but he did. He grew up in Detroit, Michigan, pretty much on the streets, and dropped out of school at the age of 16 after he'd had a massive barney with his mum. I know what that's like because I've had quite a few with Linda Bear, but I've never gone out in that much of a huff because I would always want my dinner. But he stormed out and never went back there, and then he ended up living on the (very cold) streets of

Detroit. I've never been homeless or anything, but I can relate to his story of feeling down and out, massively.

Now I've got some money and I'm feeling motivated again, I'd like to go back to Australia next year – I think I'll do PAs and tour around the country. Australia will always have a special place in my heart and I can't wait to get back there.

As far as cars are concerned, I feel I deserve Batman's car because I used to drive my brother Robert's van. I had started driving it to work – for two or three years I drove that van. I loved the van. I used to bang birds in the back of it. It was fun, but when I came out of the shower looking clean, all nice and fresh, and got into the van – it just didn't go with the look, the image I wanted. I just felt grubby again. It was also always cold and it stunk because I had spilled oil in the back. It was a bit embarrassing. So as far as my dream car goes, I've just bought my first car in five years. It's a Mercedes convertible with heated seats – oh my God it's so lovely, and my bum feels so warm. It's definitely an upgrade from my van; in the Mercedes, you press a button and the roof goes down – the van definitely didn't do that. It's so nice now to have a shower, put clean clothes on, and then get into a clean car. It's the best feeling. It's got a special number plate, stitched-in head rests and I put neon lights underneath so when I drive about it looks like I'm driving a spaceship. My car is outrageous, but I love it; I never, ever, ever want to sell my cars, I want to collect them. Batman had loads of cars, so why not me?

The Merc's not the limit, my ambition with cars is to own a bright green Lamborghini – that would be the absolute SHIT. Can you imagine me in one of those? I want everyone to hear me wherever I am and everyone to look at me and think, "Yeah alright, you flash cunt." But they won't know that I've been given nothing and worked extremely hard to get everything that I have. I'm going to be so grateful when I get these nice things because it'll show that you can come from nothing and have what you want if you work hard enough.
I just want it all, man. And I think more than being flash, it's to show that I'm proud of what I've achieved. If you're a bit flash here and there, I think it's okay if you're not being a wanker with it. My brother Danny is the perfect example of showing you've done well for yourself and being proud of it, but not too proud. After starting out with nothing, he now drives around in a Bentley convertible. He gets to do that because he's achieved so much. So, if you want to put loud music on in your car, do that, you've earned it. Thing is with Danny, he's not actually "flash". He's got a business mind, he does his thing, and he's got the nice life to show for it. He buys properties but doesn't flaunt it; he is very humble about that sort of thing. He could blow so many people out of the water with all the money he's got, but he doesn't bang on about it (I do). I think having a nice car to make you feel good about what you've done is just something people like Danny deserve.

BEARZY'S TOP TIPS ON AMBITIONS

The only thing you need to know is from the first motivational speech that I listened to by Dr Eric, which was this from his *Secrets to Success*. Every word of it made sense to me. Even now I get so fired up when I listen to these chats on YouTube – everyone could do with a bit of it. I was listening to this one going to myself, "Come on Bear, you can do this, you can win at life."

When I tell you about the story of "the young man who wants to make a lot of money", you might not be surprised to know I used to imagine myself as him. This is how that story goes:

There was a young man who wanted to make a lot of money. So he goes to this guru and says, "You know, I want be on the same level you're on." The guru says, "If you want to be on the same level I'm on, then I'll meet you tomorrow, at the beach at 4am." The young man's like, "The beach? I said I want to make money. I don't want to swim." The guru replies, "If you want to make money, I'll meet you tomorrow. The beach. 4am."

So the young man arrives at the beach at 4am; he's all ready to rock 'n' roll and wearing a business suit (but as you'll find out, he should have worn shorts …). The old man grabs his hand and says, "How badly do you want to be successful?" The young man says, "Real bad." The guru says, "Walk out into the water."

The young man follows the guru's instructions, walks out into the water and goes in waist deep. He thinks, "This guy is crazy. I wanna make money and he's got me out here swimming – I didn't ask to be a lifeguard. I wanna make money." But the guru says, "Go out a little further." The young man does as he's told, and walks out a little further. The water's right around his shoulders now, and he thinks, "This old man is crazy. He may be making money, but he's crazy." The guru says, "Come on, out a little further."

The young man goes out a little further – the water is right at his mouth – and my man's like, "I'm not about to go further in. This guy is out of his mind!" The guru hears him and says, "I thought you said you wanted to be successful?" The young man says, "I do." So the guru replies, "Well, walk a little further." And as he says this he goes into the water, pulls the young man's head into the water and holds him down.

The young man starts getting angry, but the guru continues to hold him down, and just before my man is about to pass out, the guru raises him up and says, "I've got a question for you: When you were underwater, what did you want to do?" The young man says, "I wanted to breathe." The guru replies, "When you want to succeed as badly as you want to breathe, then you'll be successful."

YES! That is the absolute BOLLOCKS. That really helped when I was feeling really fucking low, and heartbroken, walking round the park for hours after splitting up with Vicky. I would walk my old dog Charlie, God rest his soul, and stick it on my headphones.

UNIT 12: SOCIAL MEDIA

*This chapter details all of the dos and don'ts in cyberspace.
It addresses how to raise your social media profile, how to
use social media as a tool to promote yourself/your company,
the psychology behind trolls and how to deal with them (and
firewall-breathing dragons).*

*Students are encouraged to evaluated their own favourite
social media apps, comparing their results with Bears; and
to share experiences of trolls and/or trolling with the class.*

BEAR ON SOCIAL MEDIA

Many people use social media for personal reasons; but
nowadays if you are not using it for business reasons as
well, you're already behind. For any business these days it's
essential that you become more popular and well known, and
social media is the perfect way to do that. Some businesses
seem to forget about social media, or think it's not really a
necessity. However, without social media, how else could
you promote your company practically for free?

Handing out leaflets, paying for adverts in papers or magazines
and that kind of thing, is just a bloody long-winded waste of
fucking money, if you ask me. I mean, think about it, how many
people will actually notice you've done it, and will it even be seen
by most of the public? No, it won't, and nobody cares anyway.

Fame is basically a business (I guess that's why they called it show business), and the answer to being successful and staying famous is social media. The main ones are: Facebook, Twitter, LinkedIn (boring one), Instagram and Snapchat (my current favourite); these are all free to use. Why wouldn't you use them? Millions of people across the world all have an account on a number of these sites. I know that some older people are often afraid to start using social media, but they are so much simpler than you would think. I reckon it's just best to get an account, log in to the site and work it out for yourself. I think it's the quickest way to learn. But if you're still a bit scared to get onto social media, or that sounds too complicated, don't worry; you can ask people for help or just google the instructions on how to use them. If you don't know how to use Google, though, you're fucked, I'm afraid. No one can help you.

But do bear in mind, even I wasn't very good with my social media for a long time, I just thought it was boring. I've got a lot better at it now, and it's good to hear what my fans are saying, and to tell people where I'm going to be when I'm out and about – doing PAs and stuff like that. Snapchat is probably one of my favourites at the moment because my life is just so funny and I like sharing the best of what's going on.

BEARZY'S TOP
SOCIAL MEDIA TIPS

Always retweet all the bad things people say about you on Twitter. It is well funny, I love it. I do try and say thank you for the good things, as well, but the funny insults are my absolute favourite. A few months ago, that girl Helen Wood, who was on *Big Brother* as well one year, said this while I was on *Ex On The Beach 2:*

"Bear, I used to think was the full package, decent looking, wind-up merchant, but then I do remember our Charlotte announcing he has a small d***, that's a shame, convinces them into bed with his motormouth but then has a dustcap for a todger. That would be my ultimate letdown, someone fit, funny, a charmer, but has a small porker, call me shallow, not bothered, I've said in previous columns, size, does, matter."

Now that is just nasty. If she wants to see my willy, she should just ask, not talk about it until she has. She is ruthless and says it just for the attention, I think. Although I'm sure she's a lovely girl when she's not being a fucking keyboard warrior. Rather than say horrible things, like Helen always seems to do, I think it's always good to keep it as happy as possible on social media; whether that's videos, photos or saying stuff on Twitter. No one wants to hear and see doom and gloom all the time – enjoy your life, be happy and show others that your life is fun. That's what I try to do, because my life actually is fun.

Another good tip is: always do some cool, sexy selfies. Choose a good filter and make sure your skin looks all gleaming and your hair is looking slick. You want to make sure lots of lovely ladies are lusting after you and printing out your photo on their HP Photosmarts at home to put on their wall, maybe. But whatever you do on the photo front, selfies or whatever else you're supposed to do with cameras, be creative by all means, but never, ever go out and put pictures of you and other reality stars on your social media. Oh my God, that is so embarrassing. Unless it's like a selfie with Michael Jackson, or maybe Frank Sinatra, honestly don't bother. If I'd managed to get a selfie with Amy Winehouse during her life, I would have definitely posted that on social media because she is important in the world. But if that person isn't, no-one cares – don't humiliate yourself by cosying up to some twat, because they ain't your friend so just bore off. Take pictures with your actual friends, who you are actually out and having a good time with; not some geezer off of *Emmerdale.* It's so muggy.

I think it's nice to have a few cool memes on your social media feed. I like upbeat positive ones, not the "my poor life, everyone hates me", "you're a bitch and I know who you are", ones – that's so lame, man.

But most of all, on social media (and also in order to be famous) you need to have very thick skin, and never let anyone bother you. The fact is, you are going to get abused left, right and centre, no matter what, so get used to it. Losers that abuse people on social media are known as "trolls". If you've not heard of these before, I'll explain what they are: social media trolls are not the wrinkly, little, pink things from your childhood with mad hair – although who knows what they look like at home? In Scandinavia, a troll is a supernatural creature that lives in the caves and mountains; on the web, a troll is nothing but a cunt. They are people who like to start a row for no reason on websites like Twitter, Facebook and Instagram by posting messages that are usually fucking horrible and rude, with the sole intent of provoking a reaction from the person whose profile it is. They want the person to get angry and, in my case, they want their fans to get angry, too. Sometimes they do this to be distracting and take focus away from something good that's happening to that person – me winning CBB, for example. Other times, they just think they are proving a point, but they are just literally shitbuckets who crave attention. So if you are the target of a troll, don't worry! It's not you, it really is them. In fact, with that attitude, you can make it fun having a troll, like I do – I actually quite enjoy it most days because the stuff they say is so shit it's funny.

But some people take it personally, and then it can be very hurtful. Some kids have even killed themselves because of trolls on the internet, and that is just tragic. I think that there are things you can do to get the troll to lose interest in you and go away. Big companies hire social media marketing companies to handle their accounts — including the trolls – because they understand that social media is a 24/7 world that never sleeps and needs to be protected from nasty little cunts with nothing better to do.

But for normal people, just by following Bear's easy tips, I can help you to get rid of trolls and restore peace on earth, and on your Twitter account:

The first thing you can do is ignore them. People troll for attention, and for the satisfaction of getting a rise out of you – it's the same reason kids throw shit-fits in Tesco, or before their bedtime when they don't want to get off their PlayStation. As with tantrum-throwing children, it can help to ignore trolls if there is only one or a few of them – deny them their life source and they are likely to go off and find some other mug to troll. However, this approach can also backfire. By staying silent you may just unleash an avalanche of trolling since no one is "reading this" anyway. Dickheads, very lonely dickheads.

If you have to respond, kill them with kindness. But often, responding to these mugs is worse than ignoring them entirely. Even if you ignore a troll, though, your friends and followers might not, and if they take the troll bait, you need to help them out. If you are famous, these are your fans after all, and sometimes you need to help them out, so try to jump in and squelch the situation before it gets out of hand. Respond quickly, hilariously and firmly. Tell them that they are very beautiful and that you'll give them a big kiss on the lips when you see them, then thank the troll for his or her opinion, and move on with your life. Hopefully he or she will piss off.

My opinion on trolls is basically this: if you've got time to sit on your computer like a big bad keyboard warrior in your jimjams with your hot milk, listening to Magic FM and slagging people off from behind your laptop, then you're a fucking sad-case and you're destined to lead a very miserable life. Enjoy!

Now, don't forget pictures of cats on your social media sites, because everyone likes photos of cats – even trolls, I believe. I like to look at #CatsOfInstagram sometimes when I am travelling. Ha ha, that hashtag is such a joke. But it's like the most famous search on Instagram, so it's not just me that really likes cats. None of the cats on there are as cute as mine, but they are all lovely little things. I do like cats.

UNIT 14: FAMILY

In this chapter we will explore Bear's ideas on family, and learn about his family and their talents, successes and quirks. Pupils will get the exclusive chance to receive life lessons from each of Bear's family members without ever having to be in his family.

Includes: Bear's parents' secret to their 35 years of marriage, how you know you've found the one and who is the cleverest out of all of his nieces and nephews.

This chapter will also teach you tips on how to deal with your own family (however annoying or unconventional) and how to really make the most of a doorbell.

BEAR ON FAMILY

My oldest brother Daniel is a complete fucking inspiration to me. When I think about what he's achieved, I feel so proud that he is my big brother. When he was 18, he went to the 1998 World Cup in France with his friend Paul Donoghue – that was the year that Glenn Hoddle (what a dick) dropped Gazza from the squad and then Gazza said he'd never play for England again. Anyway, back to the point. Danny wasn't going there for anything other than a laugh and to watch the football; but while he was out there he saw a few amazing French bakeries with all different types of bread (not just baguettes and croissants, but really amazing stuff that he'd never seen before). He was struck with this idea: the bakeries had far more selection than you get in the UK, so he thought, "Why isn't there anything like that in England?" Bread is something that most families eat every single day; so why not throw a selection into the mix and make a killing from it. At the time, Danny was working as a barrister, but he really thought he could make this idea work. So one day, he went to the head barrister and said, "I need to borrow some money to open up a coffee shop …" he told the head barrister exactly what his vision was, and the guy said yes!

Obviously, setting up the business took a lot of planning – a lot of research, and so much work – but he eventually opened it up and called the shop Euphorium Bakery. It did really well from the off, and soon, it was doing so well that he opened up a second shop, then a third. All of a sudden he had ten shops – obviously he'd paid all the money back to the head barrister by now, and made bundles more. Then one day, someone from Tesco went into Euphorium and said to him, "We need to have your bakery in Tesco." They were serious: they wanted a Euphorium Bakery in every Tesco Extra in Britain. So, before he agreed to anything, he did his homework again, weighed it all up and then made his decision. He ended up selling his bakery to Tesco for millions. There's a Euphorium Bakery now in every big Tesco you go into, all started by Danny. He is unbelievable at business, but he didn't have any university training or anything like that; he used to work on a stall with my dad and that's how he got the hunger for making money. He's proof it doesn't matter where you come from, you can succeed.

As soon as I left the *Big Brother* house, everyone was calling my name and I could've gone off the rails, but I got in the car with Danny, and he gave me another amazing piece of advice – maybe the best, because he knows the potential I've got to go on random wanderings and he thinks I can be silly. His advice was, "You've got one chance at this, so don't fuck it up. Everyone wants you to fail, everyone thinks you're going to take drugs, everyone thinks you're not going to turn up to work on time. Now is your chance to prove them all wrong." And he was right – just prove everyone wrong and eventually people's opinions will change. It's going to be hard but, he said, "Don't be one of those weak people who give in to drink and drugs, and go to parties. Because, at the end the day, those sort of people all want to see you fail. They're all petty, slagging you off behind your back." His eyes were red and he seemed a bit sad; a bit worried about me. He'd actually travelled all the way from Italy, he'd left his wife there to come back and give me that advice. That's special.

The next morning, that advice was stuck in my head. I was on *The Saturday Show* but it was all I could think about. Danny's a millionaire, he owes me money but he doesn't give me a penny, and I used to hate him for that. It was a bit frustrating at times, but it did mould me into the person that I am today. And when he gave me that advice, it was like a caring side to him. Afterwards, he said, "You've done well. I'm really proud of you." That was really nice of him, because he never says things like that.

My sister, Hailey, and I get on well. I shared a room with her until I was 11; she's eight years older than me, so that must've been quite tough for her at times. She always looked after me when we were younger. She'd work in her office job, but would always find time for me: she'd take me out for food, sit with me and play. She was a great big sister. I think I've got exactly the same thinking as her, probably because she taught me a lot about girls: how to speak to them, how to treat them, how to look after them – all that came from Hailey. Growing up and having her drum it in to me made me who I am in relationships (so blame her). For example, when a girl texts you, don't reply straight away; just wait. She also taught me that even if a girl offers to pay for dinner, never let her pay. Never. These are the sort of things she taught me – it was the best knowledge to get. But I thought all guys behaved like this, and apparently they don't. I say to my friends, "What kind of man are you to go halves with a girl on dinner?" It gives me the hump. I wouldn't embarrass myself like that. If a girl starts going through her handbag for her money, I say, "Don't embarrass me darling." Unfortunately, that's probably why I am always skint. Still, as a man, I believe you should be the provider.

But I know that Hailey was very worried I would change as a person after coming out of *CBB*; that I would neglect the family or something because when I first got out I was so busy with work that sometimes I would miss a text. Now I know Hailey can take this as a personal insult, so I ring her or just go and see her spontaneously. I get the kids lunch and do stuff like that. She's too embarrassed to ask for things sometimes, but I'll never let her down. Every time I get some money, I just want to make sure my family are sorted out and okay, I think that's the right thing to do. I could die tomorrow; I want to know I did things properly. Life is too short, you should help the people around you straight away, it's cleansing. I've had a lucky break and I'm going to make sure that no one has any money issues in my family ever again.

Robert is my closest sibling in age; he's two years older than me. Rob loves me so much. We grew up together playing on the streets – he was only two years above me at school, so we always knew each other's friends. Rob seems like the quietest in the family (not when you get to know him, though), and with strangers he needs a little encouragement. When we go into a club, I always say to him, "Look Rob, you'll never see these people again, the worst thing a bird can say is 'no' and you'll never see her again." Now it's getting ingrained in him. And I've got him onto Twitter, Instagram and Snapchat since I've been out of *Big Brother*; now he's getting loads of attention. He reckons he didn't need it, but I always tag him in stuff, and he's got so many birds these days he doesn't know what to do with them all. He's giving it large – I do videos of him kissing girls, and his confidence levels are much better.

My family and I always dig each other out, but now, he's the Sheriff. He just needed to be livened up a bit. He worked for my brother Danny for a while, who instilled into him that "no-one owes you anything in life", which is right. So it's now dawned on Rob that the world doesn't owe him anything, and it's what he does that counts. He needs the hunger, like we all do – it's a mindset thing. When Rob gets his teeth into something, he gets it done properly, like he's in "OCD zone" or something. Once he's in that zone, he does things to a tee; he is brilliant. I'd like him to be director of my company East End Clobber, because

I think he's brilliant when he's super motivated. Would he like his younger brother as a boss? Yeah, of course – I bring out the best in people. All you have to do is follow these simple rules: don't wake up late, get out of bed, and just make it happen. There's always someone out there that would love to be you, able-bodied and well, so never forget that. I never wanted to be one of those people than turns around at 30 and thinks, "What did you do with your life?" Let's have it.

My mum and dad have been together for 35 years. They are what marriage should be about, in my opinion. What I mean is that when two people love each other, that's it, for life. You have hard times, of course you do, but it's how you stick together through it all that makes it so special. They've had money troubles; had to learn to budget and just deal with it. All the little squabbles they just put behind them. They've always taught us to appreciate what we've actually got, and to realise how hard some people really do have it.

I never shock my mum and dad with anything I do, because the kind of people they are, they don't mind what I do or who I bring home. They've said to me things like, "What's her name then, Tuesday?" I'm always texting different girls when I'm single; and at the moment, I'm a bit scared of commitment. It makes my dad laugh so much to hear my stories of meeting different girls. One time, I was having sex with Vicky Pattison in my room at home, and we could hear this weird clicking sound; we stopped, "What's that noise?" she said. It was my mum cutting her fucking toenails in the bathroom. Vicky and I were laughing our heads off.

mum is
doing the
gardening

Dad walking round
the park.

I think that once you know that someone is "the one", well, you just know. My mum has always said that once you have kids with someone, you need to stick with them because it gets so complicated and confusing for the kids otherwise. You just have to enjoy each other's company and make things work – I know that's a bit of an old-fashioned way of looking at things but I understand what she's saying. Fortunately, Mum and Dad, do enjoy each other's company, and are still madly in love – they celebrate their anniversary every year, and Dad takes her out whenever he can. I think it's amazing. Find the right person and dedicate yourself to them; if it ever gets tough, it's only ever a case of working through things. To be fair, there's a lot more distractions these days with social media and stuff like that; but the grass isn't always greener, even though a lot of people make the mistake of thinking that. Back when Mum and Dad got together, they didn't have an iPhone to distract them, so they paid more attention to each other, and I think that's a good thing. I think couples now waste so much time just staring at their phones, not even speaking to each other, which just means that they hardly know each other all. It's a shame, really; my mum and dad got to know each other inside out, I think all of their generation did.

When we're all together as a family, everyone is always trying to out-do each other in the "loudness stakes". Dad is probably the loudest – in Mum's defense she doesn't say much at all, she just cooks a bit of dinner and let's us all get on with it. But she is very funny and witty, she just digs everyone out subtly. But yeah, my dad is the loudest, and everyone loves him. He is off his head, an absolute lunatic. He dresses up as Spiderman for fun, and walks around the park talking to people and chatting to the neighbours. He's got about 100 hats and he likes to try and wear them all at once.

I'm not a dad yet, but I am an uncle, and have quite a few nieces and nephews from my brothers and sister. My first nephew is Harrison, who is seven. He's my brother Danny's son. He is very clever and not into football, which annoys my brother, but Harrison just prefers playing with toys – fair enough, in my opinion. He's got Spiderman, Pokémon, toy cars and he loves Mario Kart on the Wii. He's also very well mannered – which is how he should be.

Faye is the cleverest of all my nieces and nephews, and she's seven, too. She's Hailey's daughter. I really don't think she should be as clever as she is. If I bring a girl round, she'll say things on purpose, like "Why are you here and not Vicky?" She knows what she's doing, too. Her memory is obviously excellent, as well. She is just really great.

Then there's Albert, who is four. He's also my sister's child. He's got a speech impediment and, as a baby, he had very bad cradle cap, which means that he now has a lot of skin allergies: he's allergic to grass, milk, bread, all kinds of everyday things. Imagine how hard that must be for him? And for my sister, of course. She works so hard at looking after him.

My sister's struggled; but she's done so well. At first she blamed herself for Albert's problems, but he's got through the worst of it, and his skin doesn't flare up as much as it used to because we know now how to avoid it. Occasionally it still happens, but he gets through it. At least he's able-bodied; there are some really sick kids out there.

Honor is the next one. She's Danny's youngest daughter. She is absolutely beautiful and gorgeous, like a little dolly. She is really cute; she's three years old and she chats a lot.

Flo is the youngest; she's 18 months old and is seriously adorable. She stands up now and smiles all the time, and when I go to pick her up she runs away from me. I was in the ball-pit with her the other day and said, "Flo Flo, give me a cuddle," but she did "the face" and legged it.

I feel broody all the time, which people don't seem to believe, but it's true. Kids are so brilliant and I would be such a fun dad. I just can't wait for my own ones. But I love being an uncle, I am the coolest ever – probably in the world. Harrison, my nephew, is the man. I am going to be the one who takes him on his first boy's holiday in Ibiza. Coincidentally, it was when my mates and I were in Ibiza, going to our hotel, that Danny rang me and said Cassie had had Harrison – "It's a boy!" (I didn't actually like his name to start with, but I do now). He will always be special because he was the first.

Harrison and Honor go to private school, so you would think they were the clever ones, but the cleverest is actually Faye. Faye and Harrison were playing a game called "find the doorbell" once – now, remember Faye goes to normal school, so shouldn't be as clever as Harrison because his school is much nicer than hers. We hid the doorbell and the kids would hide outside, then when they came back in, they had to find the doorbell. I know it sounds like a bit of a shit game but they are little kids and they loved it. When the two of them played it, Faye won every single time; my brother Danny was getting the right hump as she's not one of his. He said, "It's over there, it's over there ..." to Harrison, trying to whisper to him so that he'd win, but he still didn't win – bless him.

For Christmas I'm going to take everyone to Haley's and treat them all to a load of doorbells. No, but I am going to buy them a lot of cool toys. If you've never been to this wonderland of a place known as Haley's, it's like the most magical, wonderful toy shop in the whole wide world – it's on Regent Street in London, and it's got seven floors with 100,000 toys on sale. This year, a trip to Haley's is going to be their big treat, and I'm going to make it extra special and dress up as an elf when I give them all their presents.

I like to treat them because things were hard at home financially when I was a kid, and they don't have to have that life because we've been blessed with a better life for them as they grow up. When I was little, we couldn't afford school dinner, so I always had to have packed lunch; but Dad did always give me £1, which was like, "Whoa ... a pound!" I felt so lucky. I used to hold it tightly in my hand like it was a £50 note made of gold (a very expensive £50 note!). I'd get a doughnut for 30p, and say to my two mates, "Do you want a doughnut?" and I'd buy one each for them, and be left with 10p. I'd come home and

Dad would say, "What did you get with your pound?" I'd tell
him, "I just bought some food, Dad." Then when I got to Year 9,
I went large and asked him for £3 a day; but he said, "No way."
Fair enough, I thought that was so much money at the time;
then he finally agreed to give it to me (legend). My brother,
Robert, got the same, but he saved up and bought a £60
paddling pool – it took him months. He felt like the main man
when he got it. He hadn't even told anyone what he was doing;
he just squirreled it away – now we call him "Mad Rob".

I'm sure Rob gets his OCD from Dad. Dad's always doing OCD-
type things, but he's funny with it. Like when he locks the kitchen
door at night, he puts a tiny bit of tissue in the keyhole. One day
I said to him, "Why do you do that, Dad?" and he shouted at me,
"IT STOPS THE DRAFT COMING IN, DUNNIT?" He's mental.
Another one of Dad's favourites is to make sure the mixer tap is
exactly in the middle of the hot and cold – he walks away, and
then creeps back round to see if the tap has moved even slightly.
He also counts the gas taps, "One, two, three, four, five, one,
two, three, four, five," leaves them and then walks back to them
to see if one has turned itself on on its own.

In his wardrobe, he has to have every single hanger one hand-
width apart. He puts his hand into the wardrobe and runs it along
his clothes to check. He goes left to right, and then does it all
over again. Then there's the clutch on his van: when he pulls up
the handbrake, he yanks it up so hard that the van starts rocking.
Then he walks towards the front door, goes back and does it
again; then he walks to the front door again, turns round and
stares at it for five minutes to check its not moving.

Every time he goes out of the house, he has got to make sure that every door upstairs is shut. Then when he shuts the front door, he bangs on the door about ten times to make sure it's definitely shut. If you have a cup of tea and put it on the coaster, my dad will walk over, take a little tissue out of his pocket, lift the cup up and wipe the coaster – then put the tea back down again! Mental.

Hailey, Danny, and Robert all have the "OCD-cleaning" trait. Danny is so bad. When I'm sitting on his sofa eating a biscuit, and holding a plate right underneath to catch the crumbs, he'll say to me, "Get that plate away from the sofa!" And I'm like, "I've got the plate underneath the biscuits to catch the crumbs!" So I find it easiest just to stop eating – but he'll still be going to me, "Crumbs, crumbs!"

Still, I think that stuff is normal now; but I appreciate other people might think it's quite strange. On Christmas Day, my dad gets drunk and puts the music on really loud, then he goes out in the garden and roars like a lion – or a bear, I suppose. He may chat to the neighbours all the time, but that doesn't mean they're best buddies. He also annoys them all because he likes to make a scene. My dad also gets kicked out of every bar he goes into – YOLO, though, anything for a little day out.

My mum gives the absolute best advice in the whole universe. My dad just wants me to be single forever, bang as many birds as possible forever, and not have a care in the world. My mum, on the other hand, wants me to find the right girl and settle down. Also, when it comes to money, she's very sensible and she gives me good advice about saving and paying off bills. I had a credit card and was two and a half grand in debt, and if I missed a payment she'd ring the people up and pass the phone to me to start making payments. Now, I'm actually debt free! I've paid everything off and a lot of that is thanks to her guidance. She's very caring, my mum, but she's a worrier – about anything: paying bills on time, making sure my car insurance is paid. And when it comes to work offers, she gives me really good advice on whether to take things or not. My mum's always got the right answer.

My dad doesn't trust anyone. His advice to me when I was a kid was, "Treat everyone as your enemy." That is the mindset he gave me from the age of about six or seven, I didn't really understand it then, but I sort of understand it now. He's right; the only people that really care about you is your family and that's it. It's sad to think like that, but it's so true, man. During my break up with Vicky, it was quite tough, but we all pulled together. If people are a bit short one month and someone needs some money, we'll pull together. And in that sense, I think it's amazing.

Someone who's basically family is my mate Mark Myers. He's been my friend since I was a kid. He's two years older than me and was in Robertshire School. Just before I went to Mexico for the first series of *Ex On The Beach*, I would go walking with Mark. We were on the same page; he lent me some money to get some clothes to do some filming with, and he never asked for it back (I paid him back anyway). And when

I was in Thailand, I could always rely on him, like if there was a phone bill and I was £60 short he would give me the money, and he hasn't got a lot of money himself. He would never be the sort of person to throw it back in my face, never. And, since I left *Big Brother*, he hasn't asked me for any money back, not one penny. All my other mates always hint about me giving them money, which I think is a bit embarrassing. But Mark's not going to mug himself off, and he's probably the only person I'd really help.

Mark's always been there, even for the little things, like when I needed a shed putting up – but he'd always say, "I don't want your money, mate, I don't want your money." Everyone else will take the £20 off me. But when they're coming to my PAs and having free drinks and I'm paying for the hotel room, taking £20 off of me is just embarrassing, for a favour. But it is what it is, it's life. But him, my mate Mark, he's the nicest of the whole bunch. I've got my family and I got Mark, and it's a bit sad to think like that, but whatever. It is what it is.

UNIT 15: THE MEDIA

This chapter will introduce you to the shiny world of the media. Over the course of the chapter, you will learn who has slagged Bear off in the media, and how great the media think Bear is and why.

This chapter will also equip students with Bear's tips on dealing with journalists, answering tricky questions, and whether it's advisable to get naked on a talk show ...

Pupils should expect to be tested on the following questions:

What is the one thing you can never ask Bear to do, unless you are the Queen?

What do journalists do just like everyone else?

BEAR ON THE MEDIA

So far, when it comes to the media, I've only had good press – they basically love me. The only exception was when Vicky Pattison slagged me off after we broke up, saying I was "the most vile and manipulative person she had ever met." They did turn on me a little bit then. But they soon loved me again when I was on *Ex On The Beach*, because it's obvious that in reality (TV) I am just harmless and funny. She can't help herself, that girl. One day, she'll find some other poor mug to focus on; but

until then, I'll put up with her nonsense about me because it is
quite funny, and it does make me feel loved.

But just because the media loves me, that doesn't mean I don't
get put down by people. I didn't know it while I was in the house,
but it turned out that during *CBB*, a lot of people were slagging
me off. No surprise that I found out about it, and who had been
saying what, when I got out. They said things like that I was a
drug-addict and a paranoid schizophrenic. Horrible things. But
I honestly thought it was funny, because I just didn't care – and
that's the best way to be. When you start responding to people
like, "How can you say this … blah, blah, blah?" That's exactly
what they want, so don't rise to it, forget about it, it's not worth
your time or energy. There are people out there that love selling
stories and want to have their picture taken just to be on the
Daily Mail Online, so they'll say anything to get a rise out of you.
Honestly, I think it's just embarrassing. I stay right out of it; I
never comment or reply if I'm getting slagged off.

So, if you're being a nice person and not slagging anyone
off, and you want to go out dressed as a killer clown or with
some nail varnish on, and if the Queen thinks it's okay –
she doesn't make some rule saying "don't do it" – I think:
go ahead, it's okay, do it. What the Queen says goes. If she
said to me, "Stephen Bear go and kill a swan with your bare
hands," well, put it this way: she is the only person in the
world who would be allowed to say that to me. Anyone else
who told me to kill a beautiful swan would get a punch in
the face, but the Queen, I must obey. I wouldn't like to do it,
of course, but if the Queen asked me I would just have to

apologise to the swan first, then kill it. I can just imagine the headlines now:

"The Queen's Signet Service!"

"Double O Swan"

"Queen Goes On Deadly Bear Hunt ..."

"Killing A Swan? It's Bearly Legal!"

"Blue Blood: It Gives You Wings"

"Stephen Bear Sadly Loses Fight To The Death With A Swan"

... I'd hope they'd be better than that, but you get the idea.

BEARZY'S TOP TIPS ON THE MEDIA

My advice for dealing with the media is to never slag anyone off. It makes you look stupid. You need to build relationships and when you go on nights out, you honestly do not need the agg of idiots coming over to you, saying, "You said this and that about me in the *Daily Star*." It's just so embarrassing. Journalists always want to hear you bad-mouth people because it's a good story for them and they've got nothing better to write about. So when you go out to an event, like a clothes show or one of those things, obviously they ask you good things; but never get tricked into slagging someone off, even if they are your worst enemy. I just say, "Yeah they're alright but enough about them, let's talk about me." That's a good tip.

The thing you have to remember about journalists is that they are just normal people who had to go school, do a poo, eat a Kit Kat – the usual. They're not aliens from another planet, so why talk back to them like they are? I like to make journalists laugh; not many people do that for them and they always seem to like it. Sometimes I ask the pretty girls if they'd like a little cuddle with me at the end, and I give them a cuddle and a little pick up off the ground. They always seem to let out a "whoop" of joy. You never really know what they've written on their notepad about you because it's all scribble, but never worry about that, as long as you've been yourself – that's all that matters. Journalists are only going to pull things that you don't want to say out of you if you let them, so just talk about how great you are and make it hard for them to change the subject.

When it comes to TV panel shows and you're on there with other guests, always try to be polite to them. It's nice to get along with everyone, especially when they are on the same sofa as you – but you need to make yourself the star of the show, which I always do. Sometimes, hosts will make you do a little activity or dress up, which is always good fun – I always tell the producers that I am literally game for anything. The other night on *The Nolan Show*, which is filmed in Belfast, I took my clothes off and so did the presenter Stephen Nolan – it was great. He is a right laugh. Most people I am on these shows with go quiet when I'm talking because they find me quite loud, but when I was on Loose Women they liked me so much, they asked me to come back the next week and surprise Sherie Hewson for her last show. It was great to do that, and I think if they ever have a male-only panel, I would be the first person to get a chair – the legendary "Loose Gentleman".

UNIT 16: BEARLIGION

This chapter will enlighten students beyond their wildest
dreams. In the subsequent pages, Bear details the founding
principles of his religion, Bearligion, and why he is qualified
to start his own religion.

The chapter then continues with Bear's seven easy to follow
commandments. Which, if put into practice, promise to turn
you into a Bearbarian at the very least (or, at most, a criminal).
Feel free to discuss this chapter among the class.

Please note: An advised "safe word" during group discussions
is "Atheist".

BEARLIGION

It may surprise you to know that Bearligion is a word I made
up myself. Bearligion is my own religion based on the things I
have engrained in myself daily. If you want to join the religion of
Bearligion, you best be aware it is a religion, not a cult – sorry
weirdos. Having a religious upbringing at school means I've had
the perfect training to start my own. I do also believe there is
someone up there; I'm being honest, there is someone there.
But I only turn to religion when I'm in trouble – if I feel ill or want
something to happen, I do pray to God. In all fairness, that's not
the right thing to do – if you're going to pray to God, why don't
you speak to God all the time? Not just when you need Him.

But that's what I do. When I was on *Big Brother,* I was like, "Please God, please let me win," or "please, please, let me get this job." Maybe, I do use God a little bit, to get things. I never really said to Him, "Oh, God, what are you up to today, hope you're all right; I hope you're keeping well." I never ask God those questions. But maybe, I'm being a bit hard on myself; I think God would be happy with me, because I do appreciate things. I appreciate my family; I don't take them for granted. I appreciate my friends, the very few I have. I appreciate clean water. Some people don't appreciate things and moan all the time. Maybe I don't speak to Him all the time, but He's looking over me and thinking, "You know what? You're actually doing all right."

For me, if you're not going to be a Bearbarian, I don't really care what religion you are, what race you are, whatever. Doesn't really bother me. I haven't got time to worry about what other people are preaching or practicing or believing in. It's not what I want to do. No one actually knows what God looks like. Some people think God has eight arms, some think he's a white man with a beard, some think he's black, some think he's a she. To be honest with you, I haven't really got any views on religion because I don't really care about other people's views. I've only got a certain amount of numbers of years in this life. I don't know when I'm going to go. I've just got to keep concentrating on me; I don't really have time to concentrate on anyone else. When you start worrying about other people and their struggles and when you invest time in them, you're not actually investing time in yourself. If you want to practice religion, go practice it, and good luck to you!

With Bearligion, you've got to believe you are the main
man. If you start following someone else, that's not cool.
If everyone's going left, you have to go right. You've got
to do things your way. It's either your way or the high way.
Don't let anyone tell you what to do. Do you know why?
You are your own person, you are an individual. Why would
someone tell you what to do? Never stand for it. That's my
pet hate. Be kind (obviously), be caring, be spontaneous.
Don't stay in the same job forever, otherwise you've lived
a boring life – you haven't grown, you've just stayed in one
position. Imagine you're a tree: you don't want just one branch
on your tree, you want to be the biggest tree with loads of
branches, and you want your brain to know everything. I want
to know everything there is to know in life. Obviously, it will
take time, but I want to see different cultures. If people are
stuck in the same job, the days are quite alike. Think about
birds, they could fly anywhere in the world, but they often
come back to the same place. I look at birds, and think how
they could fly anywhere in the world, but they stay here.
Then I think to myself, "You've got to think you're a bird.
You can go everywhere, so why don't you go everywhere?
Don't stay in the same place."

If my religion had a holy book, there would be lots of pictures
in it. And those buttons where you press them and they make
noises; and once you open a page it's like a pop-up book – the
best of all books. To follow Bearligion, all you have to do is read
this book and do what I do. Instead of being a "Christian" I will
call you "Bearbarians" like "Bar-barians", but more cuddly and
fluffy, and with better clothes and trainers … and manners.

I take my inspiration for Bearligion from every part of life: maybe a walk in the park or on stage at a PA or in my bedroom at home. I am always writing things down and drawing; never stop recording your ideas because even if you don't use them immediately, when you go back to them, you can often get more inspiration and strike gold with an amazing business idea.

The central part of Bearligion is that my way is always the right way, always – a lot like a fascist dictatorship. I recommend that everyone follow my advice, because taking my advice has worked pretty well for me so far.

My rules to live by are as follows:

THOU SHALT ALWAYS BE CLEAN AND SHOWERED

Some people might say this isn't a rule, but rather habits practiced by the majority of civilised society. But still, you have to make sure you smell nice and brush your teeth, because you never know who you're going to meet. I don't mean to arrogant, but you just never know who you are going to meet when you go outside, so stay fresh at all times. It's also good manners to smell nice for other people, as well. In my opinion, if you look nice, you feel nice, and it's when you feel nice that you conquer the world.

THOU SHALT ALWAYS STAY ACTIVE

It doesn't matter what you are doing; you need to keep fit. When I have a workout, I always feel better afterwards because it gets rid of any anger or stress. You turn your phone off, go to the gym and come out thinking to yourself, "What was I worried about again?" It is the best therapy ever and it puts you back on top. You turn a negative into a positive just by going to the gym, and I love it. I've just started boxing again and that makes me feel unreal after a session. When I get my head in the zone, start eating properly and looking after myself, I feel so good, and so will you!

THOU SHALT ALWAYS WEAR INVISIBLE SOCKS

Speaking of staying active, wear invisible socks when you're out and about. I hate people who wear trainers with white socks. A black trainer and a pair of white socks, for me that's one thing you just don't do.

THOU SHALT MOVE OUT OF HOME

Move out. Just do it. You need your own property. If you live at home forever you're not growing, you're not trying. I think you need a property because that property is yours alone, and that's where you start your family. You take your wife there, you get your wife pregnant, you have kids. You can't have kids in your childhood home – it's not the be-all and end-all, but personally I don't really want to start a family in my bedroom.

THOU SHALT BE YOUR OWN BOSS

Well, let someone else be your boss first, learn your trade inside out, then take all your boss's contacts and do your own thing. Whatever your trade is, the best thing in the world is working for yourself because then you can be in charge of what you do, and then the sky is the limit.

For a start, you can make loads of money if you're working for yourself, and having money means freedom. It doesn't happen overnight, but it will happen if you work hard and are willing to make sacrifices. For example, don't spend your £100 going out for the night and getting drunk, save that £100 and go to bed early; put the money towards your business idea instead.

But maybe you don't feel like doing that until you've been young and had loads of fun already, then want to start being sensible (I used to get my money and blow it). Then, like me, you get to 26 and think, "I need to get property, I need to settle down." You need to take control of your life and work out what is important and what isn't. Is going out and getting drunk still important to you, or is holding on to money and focusing on the rest of your life? You've got to stop sometimes and think about your priorities and get them straight. Some people just don't take control of their own lives early enough and it slips away from them. I learned all of this from Danny. He is the master. He knows how to treat people and he knows what to do when people are unfair to him; he also looks after the people who treat him well and show their loyalty.

THOU SHALT BE NICE TO EVERYONE

Another thing Danny taught me is that when you fight fire with water, the bad people get confused. When I wake up in the morning and look in the mirror, I say, "Stephen Bear, just be happy." So that's what I do, regardless of the other wankers. But saying that, never let anyone take the piss out of you. If you're being nice to someone and they go and mug you off, walk away from that person in a heartbeat and never talk to them again. Ruthless? Sure, but that's what I do. If I don't want someone around me because it doesn't feel right, they've just got to go. Don't let it build up and wait, just cut them off.

THOU SHALT GET A PET

Get a dog. A dog or a cat. I'll tell you why, because they are caring and it lifts the mood, it really does. When you come home from work after a long hard day, you're going to stroke your cat, stroke your dog. It will release endorphins. It does for me, it does for everyone, and endorphins make you happy – that's science and religion combined. There aren't many religions that can say that, are there?

THOU SHALT LEARN HOW TO COOK

This one is simple: no one likes to be with someone who can't cook. Just get the frying pan out and start practicing. (And actually, while you're at it, learn how to use the washing machine. I haven't really practiced that rule yet; I haven't got a bloody clue. I am going to ask my mum, though; I need to know how to do it – we all do.)

THOU SHALT SHOW STRENGTH
AT THE RIGHT TIMES

Put your foot down if someone is taking advantage. No being nice then, just sort it out yourself before it gets any worse. If someone mugs me off, I drive down to wherever they are and sort them out myself. I don't do it aggressively; it just means it's done face-to-face in an honest way. You know how I feel, I know how you feel – you get to the truth straight away, no hassle. I think that's the way you've got to be.

THOU SHALT NOT JUDGE OTHER PEOPLE (UNTIL YOU KNOW THEM YOURSELF)

If your friend doesn't like someone, but that person has always been fine to you, don't just hate on them because your friend does. Rumours aren't cool, either. Some of my very best mates have been people that no one else had the time of day for until they starting knocking round with me – I often make not-popular people quite popular. Not because I'm being big headed in any way, just because I genuinely like them. When someone is cool but they don't know it, try and bring the best out in them and nurture them like a tiny flower. Then you get to see them grow into something very special, and you'll honestly get such a massive kick out of how much you helped them – it's like having kids but with less headfucks and nappies (hopefully).

THOU SHALT ASK YOUR MUM FOR ADVICE

If God's busy with other calls and not replying to you, ask your mum for advice. She knows.

THOU SHALT WORK HARD

This is my final commandment. As Danny always says, "No-one owes you anything in life." This is something that I'll pass on to my kids, too. When they get to 18, I'll sit them down and say, "What do you want to do?" Whatever they say, I'll go, "Right I'll help you, and we'll set this up together." My dad didn't do this for me, but it's definitely something that I'll do. I'm not going to just give them a flash car or a flash house – what does that teach you? Just to sit in bed all day and ponce off your rich dad for money. There is no way I would let that happen. When I have children, they are going to be raised the right way and do jobs for pocket money from as young as they can.

So, there you go. Those are the rules for Bearligion. You can either take them with a pinch of salt, or become a fundamentalist; that, dear Bearbarian, is up to you.

UNIT 17: THINGS YOU NEVER KNEW ABOUT BEAR

This chapter is dedicated to improving your general knowledge about Bear, and your all-round Bear (and life) expertise. If students have ever wondered who the most over-rated musician is, whose shoes Bear dreams about or how to win arguments, they will find the answers in this chapter.

Features: A special letter from Bear to his 16-year-old-self, which students can apply to themselves, at any age.

Pupils should expect a "general knowledge exam" on completion of the book. Once this has been completed, students should go out and celebrate their successful completion of the course.

Please note: *Students are advised to celebrate responsibly, and within the confines of the law.*

THINGS YOU NEVER KNEW ABOUT BEAR

I like to think of this chapter as the "bonus chapter", because it's all the little tidbits you'd never know about me otherwise. Most people think I spend basically all my time out on the lash, but that's not true at all. I am a man of substance in many ways. Here I've compiled just a few of the many reasons why I am both a man of substance and a man of culture:

TELEVISION

I don't get to watch very much television these days because I'm so busy; but when I do, I love watching *Family Guy*. Occasionally, I have time to get into a series. The best one I've seen on Netflix is *Narcos* – that was amazing viewing, Pablo Escobar was a true entrepreneur.

I liked telly a lot more when I was younger. I used to watch *Teenage Mutant Ninja Turtles* – you know, the heroes in a half-shell. My favourite was Michelangelo; he was the party dude and wore the orange mask. On my birthdays, my mum used to make these wicked Michelangelo cakes for my parties, they were the best thing ever. She is an absolutely brilliant cook, just so clever at making stuff like that. I also liked *Power Rangers* – the white one was the best. And the *Power Rangers* film? That was SICK. On Saturday mornings, I used to watch *Rugrats* and *Wacky Racers* – with Dick Dastardly and Muttley the dog. I think that show was probably my favourite, actually. I loved the two stone-age guys who used to hit each other with clubs; I loved them. When I got a bit older and we got Sky, I watched every single episode of *The Simpsons*; Bart Simpson was the absolute man – probably one of my big inspirations in life. I still love *The Simpsons* and sometimes watch it when it's on, but there isn't one I haven't already seen and laughed my head off at.

MUSIC

When it comes to music, I just like what I like – and that's what I like. I used to listen to Frank Sinatra a lot because it's what my dad plays non-stop, so I grew to like it, too. Sinatra was one very cool cat. My dad used to put Frank, the legend, on the stereo, and have the TV on until very late at night; Mum would inevitably come down, absolutely raging, pull the socket out the wall and shout, "Go to fucking bed." He still plays it on full blast now – after a few drinks, he doesn't care what anyone says and belts out *My Way* whenever the mood strikes him. When I was a kid, the sort of music I used to love was Wham! *Wake Me Up Before You Go-Go* was definitely my favourite tune. Not only were the tunes great, but so were the haircuts, the fashion and the general swag. I thought George Michael always looked really slick, and *Club Tropicana* was probably my first experience of seeing the Hawaiian shirt looking fucking excellent on someone.

I like to be diverse with music (and many other areas), so Wham! is a lot different to the stuff I listen to now. Some days, I like a lot of grime: Skepta, Lethal Bizzle and sometimes Dizzee Rascal. Other days, I like deep house because it reminds me of Ibiza, and clubbing in general; so I put that on when I want to have a good dance or just reminisce about wicked nights out from the past. I also love 50 Cent and I absolutely love Amy Winehouse. What a loss her death was; I mean, the most tragic loss of life I can think of. She was in a totally different league, in my opinion. All of her music makes such sense to me, not just when you hear her songs, but also when you see it all written down and take it all in properly on the page – she was a genius. Forget John Lennon, he was overrated; Amy Winehouse knocked that stuff out of the park. I've watched that documentary they made about her a few times now and I've got the DVD at home. Her performances are just jaw dropping, how can anyone have been that musically inspired at such a young age?

But when I'm drunk, I still listen to *My Way*. I wonder where I picked that little habit up?

FAME

I'm so lucky. I obviously had a bit of a taste of fame doing *Ex On The Beach* the first time around, and all of a sudden I had a lot of people around me, but then they all disappeared. The next time, when I went to Thailand, my whole mindset was different; and then *Big Brother* came calling, so it was like a double whammy of exposure – but by then I was so mature, and I'm only 26. I now know who to help and who to not, and who to have seen around me, so I just feel so lucky.

My thinking has saved me a lot of money now; like a hell of a lot of money. I'm so ruthless now, I won't even lend someone a grand, because I work hard to earn this money and some people think it's easy. For example: I finished filming at half nine yesterday, I finished at two in the morning the night before; yesterday I got home around ten and just said goodnight to my family, woke up today at eight and I've already fitted so much into today. It's because I work hard – I'm constantly at work, work, work. People think it's easy, but it's not. I'm just so hungry for it. I'm not getting tired; I'm too excited about what's coming up.

Fame is hard work, but it can be very helpful in getting you out of tricky situations. For instance, I've got a new number plate on my car. It reads "8" "E" "A" "R" (BEAR – get it?). I spent four grand on it, and four grand is a hell of a lot of money. Well, to me it's a lot of money. But I thought, as I'm working hard for it, why can't I treat myself? So I got that plate and registered it to my car … at least, I thought it was registered. The next thing I know, the police have pulled me over because it turns out that the plate my car was insured with is my old number plate – I hadn't got my new number plate registered to it because I hadn't gone through the process properly (whoops). So they pulled me over, and the policeman said straight away, "That's a £60 fine." Then he started looking at my window tint and said, "That's another fine," and they could've taken my car off of me. But because I was Bear from *Big Brother* and *Ex On The Beach*, they ended up laughing at my jokes, and I ended up having selfies with the policemen. That is unheard of. It just goes to show a bit of fame does help sometimes.

FILM

When it comes to films, I like Disney … a lot. *Hercules* and *Aladdin* are my favourite of the Disney films; I know all the songs on *Aladdin.* I like Disney films because they're just so happy, and what idiot doesn't like happy? I love seeing everyone at home watching with big cheesy grins on their little faces. I do like horror films as well; but most of all, I like films that make me feel something, whether it's happy or sad – just thought provoking, I suppose. That's probably why I also love all the incredibly thought-provoking *Rocky* films, and the story behind them (seriously). When Sylvester Stallone was starting out, he had no money, and he went from agent to agent to try and get someone to buy the script, but no one would. He didn't stop, though, he didn't give up; he pounded the streets getting knock-back after knock-back. But he kept going out there and knocking on doors because he just believed in the script so much. Eventually, someone did take it on, and the rest is history. Imagine how all those people who refused him felt once it became a huge success? Gutted, I hope. That's the kind of belief that I want to have in my work – to inspire me so much that I'll never give up on any project that I really believe in.

I like a lot of actors, Sylvester Stallone included, but my all-time favourites are Al Pacino, Robert De Niro and Johnny Depp, because I love *Scarface* and *The Godfather* films – that kind of thing – and I think Johnny Depp is just so cool and different.

HEROES

Most people take the piss out of me when I tell them who my idols are, because I sound like a six-year-old on stage at a holiday camp, but here goes: the first one is Michael Jackson, he was also a genius. I loved his dancing, his singing, his style. He's a part of history now, and he was everything to me when I was growing up. A lot of terrible things have been alleged about him and, honestly, who knows the truth? But it doesn't take away from the fact that he was a guru of music who will never be forgotten by anyone (except maybe a few people in some remote Amazon tribes who never knew who he was but, you get my point).

My other main idol is David Beckham. I used to look at him on telly or in the paper when I was little and think, "Whoa, he's so cool." I loved the way he changed his hair all the time; I'm sure he's the reason I do the same to mine all the time now. I used to love his football boots, too; he had a pair of these Puma Kings boots that I will never forget – I used to dream about those boots. Also, he's just a great guy, isn't he? He's a wicked dad and a great husband, and he loves his family – I don't think anything makes a bloke more of a hero than that. Plus, I've never seen him look anything buy totally stylish – he's got a gift for football and a gift for looking immaculate. Hair Gel Beckham. I remember I bought some blue cream because his face was on the actual hair stuff itself. I only started doing my hair because of David Beckham. I wanted it like his: sleeked back.

HOME LIFE

I do try and help my mum around the house as much as I can, but at the moment I'm not helping very much at all because I'm sorting out my wardrobe, which means there are black bin-bags of clothes in literally every room of the house. My mum is currently going mental at me every day about it – I don't really know why, it's not like I am leaving bags of actual rubbish around the house. I'm also trying to decorate my room, but there's loads of stuff in there that I need to sort out, as well. Unfortunately, I'm just too busy all the time taking over the world.

I am also a good cook, when I'm allowed in the kitchen. I make chicken curry with rice as my signature dish. The recipe is: get Uncle Ben's rice and put it in the microwave for ten minutes, then I do the rest because it's a secret recipe. I'd really like to make *Celebrity Masterchef* the next show that I do; I would love to make something that blows my mum's mind – and before I do that with a baby, I'd like to start with a consommé.

GOING OUT

Before, when I used to go out, I was so pathetic. A few hundred quid was a lot of money back then, but the other night I was out with my cousins and my friends, and obviously I got the table so I had to pay for it. From the outside it doesn't look like you're spending a lot of money on those tables, but you are. We were drinking vodka and I was spending £375 a bottle – obviously there are more expensive vodkas, but I end up getting four bottles. I just wanted to blowout. And the next day when I woke up, I thought, "This is actually quite a nice feeling." I've basically done nearly a month's salary of what I used to earn on one night to chill out with my friends and family; that's what I appreciate. I'm so lucky to be the position I am in. Some people get their money and spank it, but that was just a rare blowout because I think it's healthy once a month to treat yourself. But only treat yourself if you think you deserve the treat. You've got to enjoy your money: you work hard to play hard, man. I think if you have a little blowout there's nothing wrong with that, if it's in moderation.

My latest night out was fucking mental. It was in Darlington and I've got it documented on my camera. It was me, my cousin Ray Ray, my brother Robert and my road manager Clinton. I've got this digital camera for my documentary and I thought I'd take it with me, too. I figured it would be a laugh on a documentary, all of us out. So, before the night started, we got three rooms – Robert in his own room, Clinton in his own room, and me and Ray Ray sharing. Ray and me were having showers, talking about life and we heard a knock on the door. I opened it and it's two girls completely off their faces on drugs – before the night had even started. Their eyes were like saucers and their jaws were somewhere else. I was like, "You alright girls?" And they said, "Uncle Bear, we found you, the receptionist told us you were in this room!" I was like, "Okay, cool." To be fair, the birds were good looking, so I said, "Come in, come in."

We ended up speaking to the girls, having a drink in the room with them, putting the music on loud. I was there chatting to one of them and got up to go and take a piss. What I didn't know was that her mate was in the bathroom and she's got coke, a lot of coke, in her hands. I just went, "Whoa, okay, this ain't my kind of party, girls, I'm sorry." It was scary, because I had the camera in my hand and didn't want to get that on film – a druggie or something. It was mad. I ended up pushing the girls out, and then I said, "I'm going to hit the club." I did a personal appearance, hit the club and started dancing in my little private area, and guess what? One of the girls came over, saying, "Bear, Bear, we're back, we're back." I was like, "Get them away from me!"

So we carried on dancing and Ray Ray pulled a bird, a good-looking girl, but it turned out this girl had a boyfriend, and he was fucking huge. Next thing I know, Ray's snogging his bird, and the bloke comes over and tries to jump on Ray. I had to jump out the way and it ended up taking five people to get him off. An hour later, the bloke was slung out the club while we were outside having a fag, and he came back again for round two. He tried to attack us again, but we managed to get back. We thought we were all cool. We had the girls back, we were going to have a good time, maybe have a kiss and a cuddle; but one girl's being sick in the toilet and the other one didn't want to sleep with me. So I was like, "This is fucking weird. You know what, girls, I'm sorry, this ain't happening. You, who's been sick in my toilet, you've got to get out." As I took the girl out, I said, "Don't be sick in the toilet babe," and the other girl jumped on me, saying, "Don't you touch my mate!" I was like, "Whoa, calm down, I'm just taking your mate outside, don't want my bathroom stinking of sick, thanks. Go in your own house and do it there if you want to throw up. I'm trying to chill out." Then it gets worse. She says the police have been called, apparently there's a bag missing. I said, "Here we go ... do you actually believe I've stolen a fucking purse? What?"

Next thing I known, I've got seven police in my room. I looked down at my belt, and I was wearing a belt that my ex-girlfriend had given me – the sparkly one, my lucky belt. So I decide to get all flash and say, "Do you know how much this belt's worth, mate? It's worth 400 quid. It's worth more than that bag, do you reckon I need that?" I wanted to show off a little bit, show I don't actually need a bloody bag. The brand of the bag was called Michael Kors. Me being me, I went, "Do you reckon I need a bloody Michael Jordan bag?" to the police. They all started laughing. Then all of a sudden, the police found the purse outside the window, and I look up and they've put me in handcuffs. I said, "Are you being serious boys? Come on, really?" Fortunately the girls didn't want to press charges and I finally got them out. But that wasn't the end of it: now the next-door neighbours then start screaming at the girls to "keep the noise down", and one of the girls ended up hitting them and the police were called again. Those girls just wanted dramas – watch out for that shit.

MOTIVATION

Things have really turned around so much for me, especially over the last year. I've had some wicked opportunities that I definitely fought really hard to get, but I've been lucky with it, too. I never used to be able to afford to go out much. I had £130 to my name last year, so it was either go out on New Year's Eve and pay a £50 bill, but then have nothing left to live on, or … well, I wasn't prepared to think of the alternative. My brother Rob was in the same boat, and we were both so fucked off about it. I remember, it was New Year's Eve and we were both just sitting there feeling so flat; so I said to him, "Right, let's write down five things we want to achieve next year." He told me I was mad, but I meant it. I've listened to so many motivational speeches walking round the park (that's right, Dr Eric Thomas) that it's been drummed into me that you can turn your life around at any point. I'd also had it drummed into me that if you write things down, you are more likely to succeed in them because you can focus on them more. So I told him it would only be five things, but those five things could change your life if you commit to them and focus. I knew that if I didn't write those things down, I'd never achieve them. So I wrote them down and made Robert do it as well on the same paper. Then I folded it up and hid it behind a photo frame of my nephew Harrison in my mum and dad's front room. The piece of paper also had my bank balance on it, which was way in the red. I put a little positive note next to it, and hid it. No one knew about it except Rob – not even my mum and dad.

When I look back at it all now, I see that it was being in such a bad way that made me so hungry for success. These days, I think to myself that from the position I am in now, I want to make a million in six months. I am going to try my hardest to do it; maybe I'll hide it behind another picture frame, who knows? I just know how hard I'm pushing with all my ideas, and I do believe that I'm in a position to do anything I want to do. I'm turning my life around and slowly it's all coming together.

TRUST

One thing I'm really big on is trust. I believe my dad is the best judge of character, he gets a feel for it, and my brother is the same. I don't know what it is, it's like some kind of magic – they just get a strong feeling about a person. I get it as well. I can tell if someone is good or bad, and I always go on gut feelings. If I feel instinctively that someone is bad, I just won't knock about with them. I'll give you an example. Suppose I'm on a big night out with a group of mates and I'm the one getting the drinks all night; I don't mind that at all, if I've invited them. But say we then get a cab home together, we stop at our destination, and they don't make the gesture to put their hand in their pocket and pay for the cab. I think that is bang out of order, and a good indication of someone's character in a big way. It's just rude, man. It may sound petty, but it means a lot, because when that happens, straight away I think to myself, "You're a cunt. Not having you around me any more." And that's that. It's the gesture, or rather lack of it.

I always offer everything, but that just shows common courtesy. To be fair, I get everything free nowadays, but say I pay for someone to get into a club, or even if I get them a job, it's just nice to know that at some point in the future, you'll get that gesture returned. Say if I want something promoted on social media and I say, "Here mate, big that up for me will you?" but they don't bother or you have to nag them to do it; I think that is bang out of order. Some people are just not decent and it's shocking – some people always have an excuse. That's why I do everything myself now. My dad always tells me, "Don't rely on anyone – no-one can be trusted other than your family. That way you never get let down."

When I was six-years-old, my dad said to me, "You've got to treat everyone as your enemy, no-one is your friend." I looked up at him and thought, "Really?" That was a lot to take in at such a young age, but it stuck with me. However, I don't follow that advice; I treat everyone really nicely, until I have a reason not to. As soon as they give me a reason, that's it – I'm fucking done with them. If I find someone even a little bit shady, I leave that someone alone – but up until I get to that point, it's all good. It can be one little thing that tips the balance and make me think, "Fuck that." I know that's a tough way of being, but I just haven't got time for it. There are enough real people in this world, and they're the ones you stick with. If someone doesn't pay you on time, you sort it out, and you know they need to be watched in the future. I don't let anyone screw me over – not in business, and certainly not in life. But you can either leave on good terms or bad terms – some people just love to slag you off and try and harm your reputation, and you have to accept that. When I've experienced that, I've just found it embarrassing. I'm only 26; where do people get off trying to have a pop at me and stop me working? They never succeed, anyway; but those people who try it are just bad to the core, I think.

I've become wiser in my thinking in the last year. Some people waste their energy being poisonous. If I were to sit there and think, "Why are they being horrible about me, what's their problem?" I'd be using all my energy sitting around all day worrying about what people think of me, and there's no way I'm ever going to waste my time doing that. I like to always be working on myself, but for me and the nice people who love me, not for someone I don't care about who's just slagging me off for attention. I think that's why I don't care what anyone says. I'm doing my thing – say something bad about me, whatever. But if you start rocking my reputation in any way, that's when you're going to be hearing from me about it.

Whenever I get someone wrong, I learn from it. Once, I was with a (well-known) girl in a nightclub, and her ex-boyfriend was already in there. I went to the table, and then her best friend walked in, too. This girl I was with then left me by myself, went into the next room where her ex and best friend were, and spent the night with them. How ruthless is that? She'd already been going down in my estimations, but she hit an all-time low at that point. Something as small as that makes me see someone's true colours. How could she have really been that into me if she'd gone and done that?

ARGUMENTS

When I get into arguments with people, I've stored up all of these bullet points as to why they're a cunt, so that when it comes to a showdown, I just shoot them out like I'm firing a gun. They're like, "Whoa, how did he remember all that?" It's because I take note of everything snaky about a person. I only argue with people I have good reason to argue with; and then I cement it in my head. That's why I value the good people around me, the little gems.

AMERICA

I'd love to travel to America. I think America would actually love me. I'm loud and I know they love that. Just before the first time I did *EOTB*, I wanted to go to Camp America and do that – I figured I could network there and meet new people. I thought it would be wicked to do loads of sports with the kids, and get them into sports themselves. I thought to myself, "It'll be like one big sports day." If I had gone, I would have saved up a bit of money first so I could stick it out, and eventually get a visa into the country. That's a dream I think I'd still like to fulfill one day.

I think my two brothers and I will probably go to Vegas at some point soon. Who knows, maybe I'll come back married to Britney Spears because she loves a bit of that, doesn't she? And she is looking really fit again now. In all seriousness, I wouldn't put it past me to end up getting married by an Elvis vicar – apparently it's mental out there, like one big playground of fun. I love American girls' accents, as well. I just think they are so, so sexy. There's something about American girls that just really does it for me – they're different to English girls, they just seem to have a bit of sparkle. They're always happy and positive, too, not like some miserable birds over here. But it's not just the birds; for some reason everyone's miserable in the UK, everyone's depressed. No one compliments anyone, or picks you up, like, "You look nice today, you look good, I like your hairstyle." But in America, everyone praises each other. Even Chloe Khan said to me that everyone appreciates her out there, and everyone says, "You look pretty, you look good." But when she's in England, people say shady comments to her – she's a bigger person than that and doesn't listen, though. Still, you've got to remember that confidence is key in America – if you've got that, they appreciate you.

ADVICE

Below is a letter I've written to my 16-year-old self. It is the best advice I could ever give him. It may sound arrogant, but it's not; it's the brutal truth. I only wish I could go back in time and deliver it. Still, no regrets. You'll be seeing a lot more of me in the future. So get fucking used to it.

Dear Stephen Henry (VIII) Bear,

This is the future you calling here, so you had better listen up! I know exactly what is going to happen, so here's what you need to do:

All that money you think you want to spend taking girls out, don't. Instead, invest it, or at least some of it, into property nice and early. The girls will always be there – they really will – and you won't be missing out by taking it a bit easier.

You will keep working, and not stop working (sorry). But if you don't invest your money, you'll never have anything to show for that work – so make that change. If you'd saved up all your money until this point, you could have probably been on the property ladder by now, so don't make any further mistakes. You might think you want to go to nightclubs with your weekly wage, spend it all on your mates and buy champagne, but you're going to regret that in the future.

As for those girls: they will have sex with you with or without the drinks, and they are only going to end up screwing you over, so leave that idea alone right now. Just stop worrying how people think you are doing. They might look at you and think, "Bear's doing alright for himself," but really you'll just end up depressed about your overspending when you haven't even got £20 to your name and you can't afford to buy a fucking peanut in Thailand. But you know what, 16-year-old Stephen Bear? If you really can't take that advice because the girls around you are too sexy not to buy drinks, forget all that; do exactly what you were going to do anyway. I'm saying this because when you do spend it all, regret doing it, feel really low and hit rock bottom; that's when you'll come back fighting and crawl your way back to the top. So fuck it, just blow all your money on crap and sort yourself from there.

It may be hard at times, but eventually you'll be glad you've been sitting in your overdraft, totally skint for so long, because it'll make you the person that you are today. It doesn't matter that you are still living at your mum's; let your mates make fun of you, because when you've got your end-game straight, it really won't matter. Just carefully make yourself a life-plan and stick to it. It may take you time, but slowly and surely you'll execute that plan and your life will be changed forever. All those people that laughed at you before will be blowing smoke up your arse and telling you how cool you are when you get there – so just sort out the weeds from the blossoms when it comes to your mates, and you'll be fine in the long run.

You also need to listen to motivational speeches. Dr Eric Thomas will change everything for you if you let him into your life.

When you see those boys in their Savile Row suits in the city, don't admire them; know that the fact of the matter is that they are all mugs. Have you heard how much they moan? They moan about getting up early, they moan about getting on the train, they moan about their paycheck and they moan about their stress levels. Why do you think that is? Because they work for someone else, of course. That's a big mistake and you'll never truly be happy doing so. My advice is to stop working for other people; scheme and plot and think of your own plan. Get your wages, don't spend your money on taking people out drinking; squirrel that money away and have a budget each week. Take a packed lunch into work and you'll not only look cool but you'll also sort yourself out quicker than you know. Just don't end up one of these moany cunts on the train to work. And don't end up with a boss you don't trust. As soon as you can strike out alone – do that.

You'll get to a day when you don't need to wake up with an alarm clock – you will work until it suits you, and you will get up when it suits you. When you are getting up to a poxy alarm at 5am and you're hating the sound of that alarm, have faith. Just know that there are better days to come and you aren't going to have to hear your iPhone ringing at the crack of dawn any more. One day, your phone will be on silent.

So get yourself out of bed, liven yourself up, work on your business ideas, and start doing what you know you are capable of doing. You'll appreciate things so much more.

Listen to Mum, Dad and Danny. They know what they are talking about. Stay ruthless, stay aware, live for the moment and trust no-one Stephen Henry Bear.

From your sexy self.

xxx

Notes

Notes